# POSH KEBABS

# POSH
# KEBABS

## Over 70 recipes for sensational skewers and chic shawarmas

Rosie Reynolds

Photography by Faith Mason

quadrille

*Publishing Director:* Sarah Lavelle
*Creative Director:* Helen Lewis
*Copy Editor:* Corinne Masciocchi
*Designer:* Gemma Hayden
*Photography:* Faith Mason
*Prop Stylist:* Alexander Breeze
*Recipe Writer and Food Stylist:* Rosie Reynolds
*Production:* Vincent Smith and Emily Noto

First published in 2017 by
Quadrille Publishing Limited
Pentagon House
52–54 Southwark Street
London SE1 1UN
www.quadrille.co.uk

Quadrille is an imprint of Hardie Grant
www.hardiegrant.com.au

Reprinted in 2017
10 9 8 7 6 5 4 3 2

Cataloguing in Publication Data: a catalogue record for this
book is available from the British Library.

ISBN: 978 1 84949 995 8

Printed in China

# CONTENTS

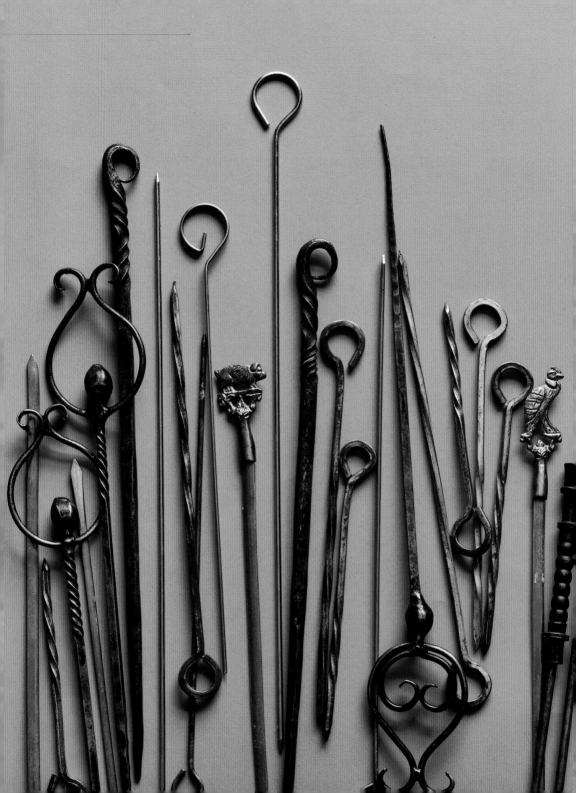

# INTRODUCTION

---

Most people would define a kebab as a dish made with roasted or grilled meat, fish, bird or vegetables, usually cooked over hot coals, and in most instances threaded onto a skewer before being cooked. But, kebabs are so, so much more than this.

Banish thoughts of the big revolving, elephant-like leg in the window of your local takeaway. This, probably the most notorious kebab of all, is known as the *doner,* and there can be few late-night revellers unfamiliar with its special charms. The name 'doner' comes from a Turkish word meaning 'rotating meat' (yes, really!). This beloved fast-food treat has acted as a lifesaver for many, a snack to soak up one's sins after a merry night on the town. But it has given the poor kebab a bad reputation. So it's high time that we posh it up.

Similarly, the *shawarma* kebab is said to take its name from the Turkish word for 'turning'. The skewer onto which the kebab of choice is threaded prior to cooking provides the name for the *shish* kebab, 'shish' meaning sword or skewer. While you queue for your kebab, you will probably have seen lines of meat- and chicken-heavy swords, ready-prepared and patiently waiting for their stint over the glowing coals.

Aside from the commonality of being skewered, turned and stuffed deliciously inside flatbreads or piled on top of buttery rice, one thing that kebabs have in common, the world over, is that they are universally loved and applauded. Eaten with glee in all corners of the globe, kebabs are evocative of good times, redolent of home, celebration and feasting.

Beyond the familiar after-hours takeaway, once you start looking, kebabs can be found everywhere, from Japanese teriyaki to Scotland's haggis kebabs to Indonesian satay.

To study all of the kebabs available worldwide could very easily become a lifetime's work! Here in *Posh Kebabs*, we've distilled that knowledge into the very best and tastiest recipes you could ever desire.

For the most tender, flavoursome kebab, it's all about keeping the meat, fish or bird as juicy as possible on the inside whilst getting the outside beautifully charred. This is usually achieved by marinating the kebabs before cooking in a host of delicious combinations of herbs and spices. Taking the time to marinate will impart great flavour to your kebabs and in many instances will tenderize the meat or bird.

The preferred way of cooking kebabs is over hot coals. But it doesn't necessarily have to be barbeque season: a griddle pan will work brilliantly if it isn't summer. For some of the kebabs in this book, there is no cooking required at all, like the fruit skewers. For others it is best to cook under a hot grill or in a frying pan where greater control can be exercised over the temperature – particularly important with some of the more delicate kebabs.

There are no rules when it comes to kebabs; they are for the most part informal food and that's why I have often specified that the kebab, whatever form it takes, should be served on a flatbread. The bread is there to soak up any juices and to act as a vehicle for sauces, salads and spreads. I like to think that it negates the requirement for a knife and fork, whilst keeping your hands clean.

Where the recipes are more formal (we are being 'posh', after all), the serving suggestions range from creamy mashed potato to dressed noodles. Like flatbreads, they are there to soak up juices and make the sum of the parts so much better than the individual components.

I've suggested salads and accompaniments wherever possible, but just like a visit to your favourite kebab house when you choose from a pick 'n' mix salad bar or decide to go with rice or French fries, or a bit of both, it really is your decision. Pile your kebabs high and serve whatever tickles your fancy.

Kebabs take people to so many places in their minds, whether the place is back home to their local high street, or to a fantastic holiday destination. *Posh Kebabs* is about bringing kebabs to the dinner table at home in a fun and unfussy fashion.

The kebab is far more than the ingredients threaded on to a skewer or thrown on the grill: it is the alchemy that occurs on the plate and the journey on which it takes you when eaten in one delicious mouthful.

# MAKING

# KEBABS

### What can you kebab?

When deciding what you will thread onto your skewers, throw on the coals, flash under a hot grill, or pile onto your flatbreads, you want to buy the best you can afford.

You are looking for meat with a slightly higher fat content than usual. You don't want an excess, but a little extra fat will help to keep your kebabs juicy when cooked at the temperatures required to get that characteristic charred exterior. When purchasing meat, grass fed and free range are the ideal.

Chicken is best if it has lead a happy life and is free range, but buy what you can afford. Where specified, buy chicken with the skin still intact – this will come into contact with the heat first and will crisp and protect the flesh, ensuring that the meat is kept tender and juicy. This is big news for both taste and texture.

Vegetables are just as important. A bag of basic supermarket carrots just won't cut it for the celebration of carrots on page 144. You want the fresh, jazzy, all-singing, all-dancing carrot tops still attached – you will know why when you taste this amazing kebab and realize how hard a humble bunch of good carrots can work for you.

Let's not forget the fish; it should smell of the sea, not fishy, have sparkling eyes and skin, and when the flesh is gently pressed with a finger it should spring back once the pressure is removed.

### Marinating

A good marinade should enhance the flavour of the meat, bird, fish, and veggies that you are cooking. You want to be able to taste both, but the meat, chicken, fish, and vegetable must be the star of the show. If it is safe to do so, taste the marinade before dunking anything raw into it; it should taste good and balanced. Be mindful that you don't want to over-season when you are marinating. Do you remember the all-important osmosis lesson in science class? Salt on the outside draws moisture from the inside, which could spell disaster for that kebab you want to be so juicy it drips down your chin.

A good marinade does require some effort, so garlic is crushed and often onions are grated and chillies finely chopped… we're trying to release as much flavour from the herbs and spices that go into the marinade as possible, so that these will be transferred into the kebabs.

Most meat and chicken will sit happily in a marinade, covered and chilled for up to 24 hours. The longer you leave the protein in the marinade the more time it has in contact with all of those delicious flavours and the more the taste will come through in the final kebab. Fish is the exception to this rule, as the delicate structures of the fish will start to 'cook' if left in anything even slightly acidic, which will affect the texture and taste of the final kebabs. As a rule, try not to leave any fish in a marinade longer than 20 minutes.

## Skewering
For those kebabs that require a skewer there are two main choices: metal and wooden. Metal are the more traditional skewers and the ones used in most kebab houses and restaurants. The advantage of using metal skewers is that they can be washed and reused. As well as this, metal skewers will conduct the heat, which helps to cook the meat from the inside. Wooden skewers are readily available and cheap to buy, however, for the most part they cannot be reused and you need to soak them in water for about 20 minutes before use to prevent them burning when placed in contact with the heat.

## Cooking kebabs
The world over, kebabs are traditionally cooked over hot coals. This method will certainly deliver the most delicious flavour and give the characteristic smoky, charred taste and appearance to a kebab that you get from cooking on a barbeque or over a fire pit. However, this is not always practical. This being the case, a good, sturdy griddle pan will work just as well. You can also cook most kebabs under a hot grill or in a heavy frying pan. Whichever method you choose, don't leave your kebabs unattended, and keep turning them to ensure even cooking.

## How to serve kebabs
The choice is all yours. Most kebabs are usually served sliced, stuffed, rolled, or folded inside some kind of bread, piled with chopped salad and smothered in sauces of your choice, from garlic yogurt to eye-wateringly spicy chilli salsa. In this book you will find serving suggestions ranging from naans topped with juicy, sticky apples; chapattis laden with spicy skewers; and lavash or flatbreads to soak up meat and salad juices. Creamy mashed potato, hot buttered basmati rice, slippery dressed noodles, crunchy vegetable noodles, and even corn tortillas. Whatever you choose to serve alongside your kebabs, remember it has to complement them, act as a vehicle for all that will be bestowed upon them, and obviously let the kebabs be the star of the show.

## Eating
The best and most important part of any recipe is the eating, and though these kebabs are all incredibly posh they will, on the odd occasion, be messy. Make sure you have a supply of napkins to hand, and where possible, eat with friends who don't mind seeing you with chilli sauce all over your chops and down your front. The best way to remove the meat from hot skewers is to hold the skewer in one hand and a fork in the other and gently push the meat off onto a plate with the tines of the fork. From then on it is your decision how you get the kebab from plate to mouth, with only one rule: you must enjoy it with huge whoops of appreciation for the cook...

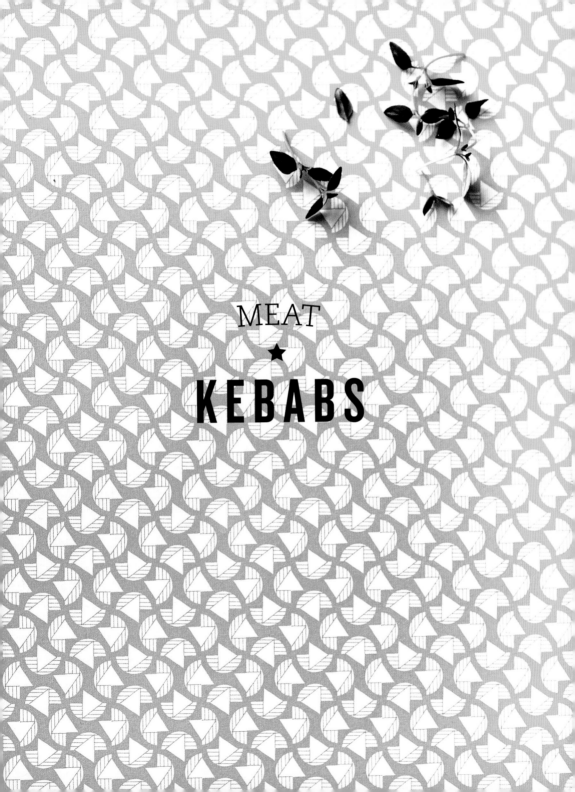

MEAT

★

# KEBABS

# MOROCCAN
★
# SPICED LAMB

Lamb skewers are the quintessential kebab. This recipe calls for lamb shoulder as it has more fat, and therefore more flavour. The spice mix is warming and exotic, and works well on all meats.

 SERVES 4

TAKES 20 minutes, plus marinating

1 generous pinch saffron
½ tsp sugar
1 tsp ground cinnamon
1 tsp ground cumin
1 tsp ground coriander
1 tsp paprika
½ tsp ground ginger
1 garlic clove, crushed
handful coriander (cilantro), leaves and stems separated
600g/1lb 5oz lamb shoulder, cut into 2.5cm/1in cubes
salt and freshly ground black pepper

In a pestle and mortar grind the saffron with the sugar until you have a bright red powder. Tip into a large mixing bowl and add 2 tablespoons warm water along with the dried spices and garlic. Finely chop the coriander stems and add to the spices with the diced lamb. Season. Stir to coat, thread the meat onto 4 skewers, then cover, marinate and chill for 30 minutes or up to 24 hours.

Heat the grill or barbeque to high. Cook the lamb for 8–10 minutes, turning frequently until the meat is charred in places and piping hot. Leave to rest for 5 minutes.

ingredients and method continue overleaf...

★ ★ ★ ★ ★ ★ ★ ★ ★ ★ ★ ★ ★ ★ ★

★ ★ ★ ★ ★ ★ ★ ★ ★ ★ ★ ★ ★ ★ ★ ★ ★ ★ ★ ★ ★ ★ ★ ★ ★ ★ ★ ★ ★ ★ ★ ★ ★

# MOROCCAN SPICED LAMB

continued...

For the couscous
200g/7oz couscous
1 vegetable stock cube
300ml/½ pint/1¼ cups boiling
  water
400g/14oz can chickpeas
  (garbanzo beans), drained
  and rinsed
50g/1¾oz roasted pistachios,
  roughly chopped
8 ready-to-eat dried apricots,
  roughly chopped
100g/3½oz pomegranate seeds
  (about 1 small pomegranate)
handful mint, finely chopped
**To serve**
lemon wedges
natural yogurt

Meanwhile, make the couscous. Tip it into a bowl, crumble over the stock cube, and pour over the water. Cover with a clean tea towel and leave to stand for 5 minutes until soft. Fluff with a fork, then add the chickpeas, pistachios, apricots, and pomegranate seeds. Stir in the mint. Transfer to a serving platter, lay the kebabs on top, and pour over any resting juices. Roughly chop the coriander leaves and scatter over the top. Serve with lemon wedges and a dollop of yogurt.

RICE & BEANS

★

# CURRIED GOAT

Goat meat is eaten throughout the Caribbean and has an amazing, rich flavour that stands up to the spices used in this recipe. You will find goat at your local Caribbean market or ask your butcher to source it for you.

 SERVES 4

 TAKES 30 minutes, plus marinating

1 bunch spring onions (scallions), roughly chopped

5cm/2in piece ginger, peeled and roughly chopped

6 thyme sprigs, leaves picked

2 scotch bonnet chillies, deseeded if you like less heat

2 tbsp Caribbean curry powder, or mild curry powder

1 tsp ground allspice

juice 1 lime, plus 2 limes, cut into wedges, to serve

2 tsp soft light brown sugar

600g/1lb 5oz goat leg meat, cut into 2.5cm/1in cubes

salt and freshly ground black pepper

Place half the spring onions, the ginger, the thyme, chillies, spices, and lime juice into the bowl of a food processor and blend until smooth. Scrape into a bowl, add the sugar and plenty of seasoning, tip in the goat meat, and toss to coat in the marinade. Thread the meat onto 4 large or 8 small skewers, brush over any excess marinade, cover and chill for at least 30 minutes.

To make the rice and beans, heat the oil in a large pan, add the remaining spring onions, and fry for 2 minutes until just starting to soften. Rinse the rice in plenty of cold water until the water runs clear, then tip it into the pan with the spring onions. Add the coconut milk, then wash out the can with 300ml/½ pint/1¼ cups cold water and add to the pan. Bring the rice to the boil, then reduce the heat, cover with a tight-fitting lid, and cook for 10 minutes.

ingredients and method continue overleaf...

★ ★ ★ ★ ★ ★ ★ ★ ★ ★ ★ ★ ★ ★

# CURRIED GOAT WITH RICE & BEANS

continued...

**For the rice and beans**
1 tbsp coconut oil
200g/7oz basmati rice
400ml/14fl oz can reduced-fat
   coconut milk
400g/14oz can kidney beans,
   drained and rinsed
large handful chopped coriander
   (cilantro), to serve

Gently fold the beans into the rice, cover with the lid, and cook for a further 5 minutes.

Meanwhile, heat a griddle pan to high and cook the skewers for 8 minutes, turning frequently until cooked through. Add the lime wedges to the pan and griddle for a few minutes until charred in places. Serve the skewers with the rice and beans, lime wedges to squeeze, and coriander scattered over.

# LAMB

★

# SHAWARMA

---

This is the sophisticated, poshed-up version of a takeaway classic. The crisp red cabbage works wonderfully with the rich lamb. Serve with a pile of French fries for a true takeaway feel.

 SERVES 6

 TAKES 2½ hours, plus marinating

1.5kg/3lb 3oz boneless leg of lamb
4 garlic cloves, crushed
1 tbsp ground cumin
1 tbsp ground coriander
1 bunch coriander (cilantro), leaves and stems separated
1 tbsp olive oil
½ red cabbage, shredded
1 red onion, thinly sliced
juice 1 lemon
2 tbsp pomegranate molasses
salt and freshly ground black pepper

**To serve**
6 flatbreads
natural yogurt
chilli sauce
pickled green chillies

Allow the lamb to come to room temperature. Use a sharp knife to make small incisions all over the surface, then transfer to a deep roasting tray. Mix the garlic, cumin, and ground coriander in a small bowl. Finely chop the coriander stems and mix into the garlic and spices along with the oil and plenty of seasoning to make a rough paste. Rub all over and into the lamb, and allow to sit for at least 30 minutes.

Preheat the oven to 200°C/180°C fan/gas 6. Roast the lamb for 30 minutes, then remove it from the oven, reduce the heat to 180°C/160°C fan/gas 4, and pour in 50ml/1¾fl oz/scant ¼ cup cold water. Cover tightly with foil and cook for a further 1 hour.

Meanwhile, mix the cabbage with the onion, lemon juice, pomegranate molasses, and some seasoning. Toss to combine and set aside until ready to use.

Remove the lamb from the oven, transfer to a board, cover loosely with foil, and rest for 20 minutes. Warm the flatbreads in the oven. Use a sharp knife to really thinly slice the lamb. Pile onto the flatbreads with the red cabbage, coriander leaves, and a dollop of yogurt. Serve with your favourite chilli sauce and pickled green chillies.

# MUTTON

★

# SOUVLAKI

The longer you leave the mutton in the marinade the more tender the meat will be and the better the flavour. Serve these souvlaki with olives, feta, and warm pittas for a true Greek experience.

 SERVES 2

 TAKES 15 minutes, plus marinating

1 onion, roughly chopped
1 large tomato, roughly chopped
2 garlic cloves
juice and zest 1 lemon, plus
    wedges, to serve
2 tsp dried oregano
1 tsp dried thyme
1 tsp dried mint
2 bay leaves
300g/10oz mutton leg, trimmed
    of excess fat, and cut into
    2.5cm/1in cubes
salt and freshly ground black
    pepper
**To serve**
handful mint
handful kalamata olives
feta
4 pitta breads
lemon wedges

Place the onion, tomato, garlic, and lemon juice and zest in a food processor and blend to a purée. Scrape out into a bowl and add the dried herbs, crush up the bay leaves, and add to the bowl with some seasoning. Add the mutton to the marinade, and toss to coat. Cover and chill for at least 30 minutes or up to 24 hours if you have time.

Lift the mutton out of the marinade and thread onto 4 skewers. Heat a barbeque or griddle pan to high and cook the skewers for 8 minutes, turning every couple of minutes, until charred in places and cooked through. Serve with mint leaves, kalamata olives, and feta and stuff into warmed pittas.

# LAMB SKEWERS

This is classic Indian takeaway fare. The tandoori
marinade will work brilliantly with chicken too;
or try it on a leg of lamb or even a whole bird.

 SERVES 4

TAKES 20 minutes,
plus marinating

3 garlic cloves, crushed
5cm/2in piece ginger, peeled and
  finely grated
2 green chillies, deseeded and
  finely chopped
juice ½ lemon
200g/7oz natural yogurt
2 tbsp sunflower oil
2 tsp paprika
2 tsp ground cumin
2 tsp garam masala
½ tsp turmeric
600g/1lb 5oz lamb shoulder, cut
  into 2.5cm/1in cubes
**For the kachumba salad**
½ cucumber, finely chopped
2 large tomatoes, deseeded and
  finely chopped
½ onion, finely chopped
handful coriander (cilantro),
  finely chopped
**To serve**
4 naan breads
natural yogurt
½ lemon, cut into wedges

In a large bowl mix the garlic, ginger, chillies, lemon
juice, and yogurt with the oil and spices. Stir to
combine, then add the lamb and toss to coat.
Cover and set aside for at least 30 minutes.

Heat a barbeque or grill to high. Lift the lamb out
of the marinade and thread onto 4 long skewers.
Cook for 8–10 minutes, turning every couple of
minutes, until the lamb is cooked through and
nicely charred in places. Leave to rest for 5 minutes.

To make the kachumba salad, combine all the
ingredients together and serve with the kebabs,
naan breads, yogurt, and lemon wedges.

# JERK

# PORK WITH APPLE SLAW

Jerk has a characteristic dark outside, while the meat remains tender and juicy in the centre – this is because the sugar caramelizes, forming a sticky, spicy crust.

 SERVES 2

 TAKES 30 minutes, plus marinating

1 scotch bonnet chilli, deseeded
   if you don't like too much heat
3 garlic cloves, crushed
3 tbsp soft dark brown sugar
1 tbsp thyme leaves
2 tbsp soy sauce
1 tsp ground allspice
½ tsp ground cumin
½ tsp ground ginger
300g/10oz pork tenderloin,
   trimmed of any sinew, cut into
   2.5cm/1in cubes
1 tbsp light-flavoured oil (such as
   vegetable oil), plus a drizzle
2 large plantain, peeled and cut
   into 1.5cm/½in slices
salt and freshly ground black
   pepper
**For the slaw**
¼ white cabbage
2 spring onions (scallions)
1 green dessert apple, cored
1 tbsp cider vinegar

Pound the chilli, garlic, sugar, and thyme leaves in a pestle and mortar with plenty of seasoning to a coarse paste. Tip into a large bowl, add the soy sauce and dried spices, then stir in the pork. Cover and leave to stand for 15 minutes.

Meanwhile, make the slaw. Shred the cabbage and spring onions, finely slice the apple into 2-mm thick slices, pour over the vinegar with the extra drizzle of oil, season, and toss to combine. Cover and set aside.

Heat a barbeque or grill to high. Thread the pork onto 2 long skewers, brushing any excess marinade over the top. Cook for 8 minutes, turning frequently, until charred on the outside and cooked through. Leave to rest for 5 minutes.

Heat the oil in a large frying pan. Fry the plantains for 2 minutes until golden and crisp, then flip them over and cook the other side. Serve with the jerk skewers and slaw, spooning over any resting juices from the meat.

# ROSEMARY

# LAMB & CANNELLINI MASH

This is one of those dishes that looks and tastes so much more complex than it actually is – say nothing and take all the credit that will be heaped on you!

 SERVES 2

 TAKES 25 minutes, plus marinating

6 rosemary sprigs
1 tbsp olive oil
1 garlic clove, crushed
4 anchovy fillets, roughly chopped
zest 1 lemon
400g/14oz lamb loin fillet, cut into 2.5cm/1in cubes
200g/7oz cherry vine tomatoes
freshly ground black pepper
**For the white bean purée**
3 tbsp olive oil
1 garlic clove, crushed
400g/14oz can cannellini beans, drained and rinsed
juice 1 lemon

Strip the leaves from the sprigs of rosemary, leaving the top bunch of leaves intact, then set aside. Very finely chop the picked leaves, then add half to a large bowl with the oil, garlic, anchovies, lemon zest, and plenty of black pepper – the anchovies will probably be salty enough, so no need for additional salt. Mash with the back of a spoon to break down the anchovies. Add the lamb and toss in the marinade. Use a metal skewer or cocktail stick to pierce a hole in the centre of each piece of meat, then carefully thread onto the reserved rosemary sprigs. Cover and leave to marinate for 15 minutes.

Meanwhile, make the white bean purée. Heat the oil in a small pan, add the garlic and remaining rosemary, and heat gently until the oil is fragrant. Tip in the beans and lemon juice, stir to coat, then crush the beans with a fork. Season, remove from the heat, and keep warm.

Heat a griddle pan to high and cook the skewers for 8 minutes, turning frequently, until charred on the outside and cooked through. Remove and set aside. Throw the cherry tomatoes into the pan and cook for 5 minutes, or until they are starting to blister and char in places. Spoon the mash onto a couple of plates and serve with the lamb skewers and tomatoes, with any resting juices poured over.

# TURKISH FLAMING

★

# VEAL SHASHLIK

Turkish peppers are a cross between a green pepper and
mild green chilli. The latter will work just as well.

 SERVES 4

 TAKES 30 minutes,
plus marinating

600g/1lb 5oz veal escalopes, cut
    into 2.5cm/1in cubes
1 tbsp olive oil
1 tsp chilli flakes
1 garlic clove, crushed
4 Turkish hot peppers, cut into
    4 chunks
1 red onion, cut into wedges
    through the root
1 medium tomato, quartered
salt and freshly ground black
    pepper
**For the ezme salad**
2 Lebanese cucumbers, finely
    chopped
2 large tomatoes, finely chopped
1 red (bell) pepper, deseeded and
    finely chopped
½ red onion, finely chopped
handful flat-leaf parsley, finely
    chopped
3 tbsp olive oil
juice ½ lemon
1 tbsp pomegranate molasses
1 tsp sumac

Mix the veal with the oil, chilli flakes, and garlic.
Season well, cover, chill and leave to marinate for at
least 30 minutes.

Thread the veal onto 4 large skewers, alternating
with the hot peppers and onion and finishing with
a tomato quarter. Heat a barbeque or griddle pan
to high. Cook the skewers for 10 minutes, turning
frequently, until charred in places and cooked
through. Leave to rest for 5 minutes.

To make the ezme salad, combine the cucumbers,
tomatoes, red pepper, onion, and parsley in a bowl.
Mix the oil, lemon juice, and pomegranate molasses
in a small bowl, then pour over the salad. Sprinkle
with the sumac and serve with the shashlik.

# RED PEPPER SAUCE

★

# AUBERGINE PATLICAN

---

Juicy meatballs are sandwiched between discs of aubergine
in this traditional Turkish kebab. The aubergines become
soft and absorb all the delicious meat flavours, and look
so fabulous reformed into their original shape. Bring
these impressive kebabs to the table with a pot of the
vibrant red pepper sauce.

  SERVES 4

TAKES 45 minutes

2 small aubergines (eggplants)
400g/14oz beef mince
2 onions
3 garlic cloves, crushed
1 tsp dried oregano
1 tsp Turkish red pepper flakes,
    plus extra to serve
handful fresh breadcrumbs
handful flat-leaf parsley, finely
    chopped
1 tbsp olive oil, plus extra for
    greasing
400g/14oz can chopped tomatoes
6 red (bell) peppers from a jar,
    drained and chopped
salt and freshly ground black
    pepper
**To serve**
natural yogurt
Turkish bread

Cut each aubergine into 5 rounds, keeping the
slices in the order they come in. Sprinkle the slices
with a little salt and set aside for 5 minutes.

Put the beef mince into a large bowl. Grate 1 of the
onions into the beef with 2 of the garlic cloves, the
oregano, pepper flakes, breadcrumbs, and most of
the parsley. Season well. Mix with your hands for 2
minutes; this will stop the meat falling apart when
cooking. Divide the meat into 8 equal portions and
shape into balls.

Preheat the oven to 200°C/180°C fan/gas 6. Pat the
aubergines dry on kitchen paper. Push a skewer
up through the base of an aubergine so it goes
through the centre, follow with a meatball, then
another aubergine slice, then another meatball,
squashing the aubergine slices and meatballs
together slightly as you go, so that the balls look
flatter, more like discs. Continue like this until you

*method continues overleaf...*

★ ★ ★ ★ ★ ★ ★ ★ ★ ★ ★ ★ ★ ★ ★ ★ ★ ★ ★ ★ ★ ★ ★ ★ ★ ★ ★ ★ ★ ★ ★ ★ ★ ★ ★ ★ ★ ★ ★ ★ ★ ★ ★ ★ ★

# AUBERGINE PATLICAN
continued...

have skewered the whole aubergine. Repeat with the second aubergine and remaining 4 meatballs to make 2 skewers in total.

Lightly grease a baking tray with oil. Lay the aubergine and meat skewers on the tray, and brush with a little more oil. Cook in the oven for 30 minutes until the aubergines are tender and the beef is cooked through, turning halfway through.

Meanwhile, to make the red pepper sauce, heat the oil in a frying pan, roughly chop the remaining onion, and add to the pan. Cook on a medium heat for 5 minutes, or until starting to soften. Add the remaining garlic, the tomatoes, and red peppers. Bubble for 10 minutes until thickened, then season to taste. Serve the sauce spooned over the kebabs, sprinkle with the remaining parsley, and eat with a dollop of yogurt and Turkish bread.

## PORTUGUESE

★

# BEEF ESPETADO

These delicious Portuguese beef skewers are so tender.
Traditionally served in bread rolls or on top of baked
polenta, however you serve them, make sure you keep
all of the pan juices for mopping and soaking up.

SERVES 4

TAKES 30 minutes,
plus marinating

500g/1lb 2oz sirloin steak, cut into
    2cm/1in cubes
100ml/3½fl oz/scant ½ cup red
    wine
1 onion, grated
4 garlic cloves, chopped
1 tsp salt
12 fresh bay leaves
knob of butter
**For the polenta**
175g/6oz instant polenta
50g/1¾oz finely grated Parmesan
100g/3½oz vine cherry tomatoes,
    halved
salt and freshly ground black
    pepper
handful chopped flat-leaf parsley,
    to serve

Put the steak into a large bowl and cover with the
wine, onion, garlic, and salt. Crush 4 of the bay
leaves and add them to the bowl, stir well, cover,
and chill for at least 2 hours; if you have time, leave
the meat to marinate overnight.

Remove the meat from the fridge, lift the beef
from the marinade, shaking off any excess juices
but reserving the marinade, then thread the cubes
of steak onto 8 small skewers, alternating with
pieces of bay leaf. Allow the skewers to come to
room temperature.

Meanwhile, make the polenta. Bring 750ml/
generous 1¼ pints/3¼ cups water to the boil. Once
boiling, stir continuously with a wooden spoon and
gradually add the polenta. Lower the heat, then
cook, stirring frequently, for 10 minutes. Remove
from the heat and stir in most of the Parmesan
along with lots of salt and black pepper.

method continues overleaf...

# PORTUGUESE BEEF ESPETADO

continued...

Spoon the polenta into a lightly greased baking tray and flatten with the back of the spoon. Dot the tomatoes over the surface and gently push them into the polenta. Cover with the remaining Parmesan and set aside. Preheat the grill to high.

Heat a large frying pan over a high heat and cook the skewers for 6 minutes, turning frequently until brown and cooked to your liking. Pour the reserved marinade into the pan along with the butter and shake the pan to emulsify the sauce. Remove from the heat and allow to rest for 5 minutes.

Grill the polenta for 2–3 minutes to melt the cheese and soften the tomatoes. Cut into slices and serve the beef skewers on top along with any cooking juices spooned over. Scatter with the parsley.

# LAMB

# KOFTA KEBABS

Lamb is naturally more fatty than beef, so these kebabs
stay wonderfully juicy when cooked over hot coals.
The onion chutney is sweet with a chilli kick and goes
perfectly with the spiced kebabs.

 SERVES 4

 TAKES 20 minutes

500g/1lb 2oz lamb mince
5cm/2in piece ginger, peeled and
    grated
2 garlic cloves, crushed
handful mint, finely chopped
handful coriander (cilantro), finely
    chopped
1 red chilli, deseeded and finely
    chopped
2 tsp ground cumin
2 tsp ground coriander
salt and freshly ground black
    pepper
**For the onion chutney**
2 small onions, thinly sliced
juice 1 lemon
2 tbsp tomato ketchup
1 tbsp mango chutney
½ tsp chilli powder
**To serve**
4 flatbreads
½ iceberg lettuce, shredded
natural yogurt (optional)

Put the lamb mince into a large bowl and add the
ginger, garlic, mint, and most of the coriander,
reserving a little for garnish. Add the chilli and
spices with plenty of seasoning. Massage with
your hands for 2 minutes; this will combine the
ingredients and help the kebabs stay together as
they cook.

Divide the lamb mixture into 4 equal portions and
using damp hands, squeeze the meat onto 4 thick,
long skewers. Grease a baking sheet with a little oil
and lay the kofta in a single layer. Set aside.

To make the onion chutney, mix all the ingredients
together in a small bowl. Season and set aside.

Heat a grill or barbeque to high. Cook the kofta for
8 minutes, turning halfway through, until golden
and cooked through. Serve rolled in a flatbread
with the onion chutney, lettuce, remaining
coriander, and a dollop of yogurt, if liked.

# KOREAN

★

# BULGOGI BEEF

Bulgogi can be interpreted as meat cooked over hot coals, or if it isn't barbeque weather, a hot griddle. Simple and satisfying, this is impressive Korean food without the need for a trip to a specialist shop.

 SERVES 4

 TAKES 20 minutes, plus marinating

3 garlic cloves, crushed
3cm/1in piece ginger, peeled and grated
2½ tbsp dark soy sauce
1½ tbsp sesame oil
1½ tbsp clear honey
¼ tsp chilli powder
500g/1lb 2oz sirloin steak, cut into 2cm/1in cubes
150g/5½oz bean sprouts
150g/5½oz baby leaf spinach
1 tbsp toasted sesame seeds, plus extra to garnish
freshly ground black pepper

First make up the marinade. In a medium bowl, mix the garlic, ginger, 2 tablespoons of the soy sauce, 1 tablespoon of the sesame oil, and 1 tablespoon of the honey. Whisk to combine, then add the chilli powder, plenty of black pepper, and the steak. Cover and chill for at least 30 minutes.

Heat a barbeque or griddle pan to high. Lift the beef out of the marinade, shaking off any excess juices, then thread onto 8 small skewers. Cook the skewers for 6–8 minutes, turning every couple of minutes until charred in places and cooked to your liking. Remove from the heat and allow to rest for a few minutes.

Meanwhile, put the kettle on. Put the bean sprouts and spinach into a colander and pour over a kettle full of boiling water. Drain well and pat dry with kitchen paper to remove any excess water. Tip into a bowl, whisk the remaining soy sauce, sesame oil, and honey, then pour over the sprouts and spinach. Toss to coat in the dressing and sprinkle over the sesame seeds. Divide between serving bowls, top with the skewers, and scatter with a few more sesame seeds.

# ARMENIAN

★

# PORK KHOROVATS

'Khorovat' means grilled, and the best way to maximize flavour is to grill over hot coals for that guaranteed smoky flavour. These kebabs taste great with the fresh parsley salad – refreshing, juicy, and full of zing.

SERVES 4

TAKES 20 minutes,
plus marinating

1 onion, grated
4 garlic cloves, roughly chopped
2 tbsp red wine vinegar
1 tbsp olive oil
2 tbsp oregano leaves, roughly
   chopped
½ tsp dried chilli flakes
½ tsp smoked paprika
600g/1lb 5oz pork loin, trimmed of
   any sinew and cut into 1.5cm/¾in
   medallions
For the parsley salad
large bunch flat-leaf parsley,
   roughly chopped
100g/3½oz baby spinach
4 spring onions (scallions), shredded
4 medium tomatoes, roughly
   chopped
1 red chilli, deseeded and finely
   chopped
juice and zest 1 lemon
olive oil, to drizzle
4 flatbreads, to serve

In a large bowl, mix the onion, garlic, vinegar, oil, oregano, and spices to combine. Add the pork and toss to coat, then cover and chill for at least 30 minutes or up to 24 hours if you have the time.

Thread the meat onto 4 skewers, shaking off any excess marinade. Heat a barbeque or griddle pan to high. Cook the skewers for 8 minutes, turning every couple of minutes, until charred in places and cooked through.

Meanwhile, make the parsley salad. In a medium bowl, mix the parsley, spinach, spring onions, tomatoes, and most of the chilli with the lemon juice. Lay on a serving platter and sprinkle with the remaining chilli and the lemon zest. Gently toss to combine, then lay the kebabs on top and drizzle with a little oil.

# SLOW-COOKED ZA'ATAR ★ LAMB SHOULDER

Cooking lamb shoulder like this, low and slow, means you get the softest, juiciest meat packed full of flavour.

 SERVES 4–6

 TAKES 4½ hours, plus marinating

2kg/4lb 8oz bone-in shoulder of
   lamb, at room temperature
3 tbsp za'atar
1 tbsp ground cumin
1 tsp chilli flakes
2 tsp ground cinnamon
6 garlic cloves, crushed
1 tbsp olive oil
handful flat-leaf parsley, leaves
   and stems separated
2 onions, quartered
salt and freshly ground black pepper

**For the chickpea yogurt**
25g/scant 1oz butter
2 garlic cloves, finely chopped
1 tbsp cumin seeds
400g/14oz can chickpeas (garbanzo
   beans), drained and rinsed
200g/7oz Greek yogurt

**To serve**
2 pickled turnips, drained and
   roughly chopped
4 medium tomatoes, roughly
   chopped
pickled green chillies
4–6 flatbreads

With a sharp knife make small, shallow incisions all over the surface of the lamb. Mix the za'atar, cumin, chilli, cinnamon, garlic, and oil together with plenty of seasoning to form a paste. Finely chop the parsley stems and add these to the paste. Rub the paste all over the lamb, cover and chill for at least 1 hour, or overnight if you have the time.

Preheat the oven to 200°C/180°C fan/gas 6. Put the onions into a roasting tray and sit the lamb on top. Roast for 30 minutes. Remove the lamb from the oven, pour in a glass of cold water, cover with foil, reduce the oven temperature to 160°C/140°C fan/ gas 3, and cook for a further 3–3½ hours, or until the lamb is really tender and pulls apart when a couple of forks are inserted into the meat.

Just before serving, make the chickpea yogurt. Melt the butter in a small frying pan, add the garlic and cumin seeds, and sizzle for 1 minute until fragrant. Tip in the chickpeas and stir to coat in the butter. Remove from the heat and add the yogurt, allowing the heat of the pan to warm the yogurt gently.

Skim any excess fat from the tray, shred the lamb using forks (discard any skin and bone), and toss with the roasted onions. Serve with the chickpea yogurt, pickled turnips, tomatoes, finely chopped parsley and green chillies piled on top of flatbreads.

STICKY MAPLE

★

# PORK BELLY SKEWERS

This pork and beans combo is great at any time of day: at breakfast with a crispy fried egg; lunch in a warm buttered crusty roll; and dinner with a hot, fluffy baked potato. Even better if you have a camp fire to eat them round.

 SERVES 4

 TAKES 30 minutes, plus marinating

1kg/2lb 4oz pork belly, cut into 2cm/1in cubes
5 tbsp maple syrup
3 tbsp dark soy sauce
1 tbsp sweet chilli sauce
1 tbsp Dijon mustard
1 garlic clove, crushed
½ tsp chilli powder

**For the smoky baked beans**
1 tbsp olive oil
1 onion, finely chopped
1 garlic clove, crushed
2 tbsp smoked paprika
1 tbsp thyme leaves
1 tsp red wine vinegar
400g/14oz can chopped tomatoes
1 tbsp maple syrup
400g/14oz can cannellini beans, drained and rinsed
400g/14oz can haricot beans, drained and rinsed

Place the pork belly into a large mixing bowl. Pour in the maple syrup, soy and sweet chilli sauces, and mustard. Add the garlic and chilli powder and mix well. Season, cover, and chill for at least 20 minutes or up to 24 hours if you have the time.

To make the smoky baked beans, heat the oil in a frying pan, add the onion, and fry on a medium heat for 5 minutes until starting to soften. Add the garlic, paprika, thyme, and vinegar and fry for a further minute. Tip in the tomatoes, maple syrup, and both types of beans. Bring to a simmer and cook for about 10 minutes until thick.

Meanwhile, preheat the grill to high. Thread the pork belly onto 4 long skewers, lay on a baking sheet, then grill for 10 minutes, turning and brushing with any excess marinade halfway through cooking until golden and cooked through.

Serve the beans alongside the pork belly skewers.

# LAMB

★

# ISKENDER KEBABS

Traditionally, Iskender kebab is incredibly rich: slices of
doner meat piled on top of pitta, smothered with a tomato
butter sauce and yogurt. Crunchy pitta soaks up all the
juices, making this dish devilishly moreish.

 SERVES 4

 TAKES 20 minutes

4 large pitta breads
600g/1lb 5oz lamb neck fillet
2 tbsp olive oil, plus a drizzle
50g/1¾oz butter
2 garlic cloves, crushed
200g/7oz vine cherry tomatoes,
    roughly chopped
2 tbsp tomato purée
2 tsp Turkish pepper flakes
200g/7oz Greek yogurt
handful flat-leaf parsley, roughly
    chopped
salt and freshly ground black
    pepper

Heat a barbeque or griddle pan to high. Heat the
pitta breads on each side for about 1½ minutes, or
until warmed, crisp, and toasted in places. Roughly
chop the pittas into wedges, then transfer to a
large serving dish.

Return the griddle pan to the heat. Once hot, rub
the lamb with a drizzle of oil, season, then cook
for 6–8 minutes, turning frequently until charred in
places and cooked to your liking. Remove from the
pan and rest on a board, covering loosely with foil.

Meanwhile, heat the oil and butter in a frying pan.
When the butter has melted, add 1 garlic clove and
the tomatoes, and cook for a few minutes over a
medium heat until they start to soften. Stir in the
tomato purée and pepper flakes until combined.
Remove from the direct heat but keep warm.

Mix the yogurt with the remaining garlic clove, then
set aside.

Thinly slice the lamb and pile on top of the crisp
pittas. Pour over any resting juices, spoon over
the hot tomato sauce and dollop over the yogurt.
Scatter with the parsley and eat immediately.

# SWEET STICKY
★
# LAMB SOSATIE

---

These sweet, spiced kebabs have that characteristic mild curry flavour so popular in Malay food. The apricot jam lends a sticky hand to their brilliance, great straight off the skewer with rice or wrapped in hot, fluffy naan bread.

 SERVES 4

 TAKES 20 minutes, plus marinating

4 tbsp apricot jam
3 tbsp mild curry powder
3 garlic cloves, crushed
3cm/1in piece ginger, peeled and grated
1 red chilli, deseeded and finely chopped
1 tbsp soft light brown sugar
juice ½ lemon
1 tsp ground turmeric
800g/1lb 12oz lamb shoulder, cut into 2.5cm/1in dice
100g/3½oz ready-to-eat dried apricots
2 onions
salt and freshly ground black pepper

In a large bowl, mix the jam, curry powder, garlic, ginger, chilli, sugar, lemon juice, and turmeric with plenty of seasoning. Tip in the lamb and toss to coat in the marinade. Cover and leave to stand for at least 30 minutes.

Meanwhile, cover the apricots with warm water and set aside. Cut the onions into quarters, then cut each quarter in half.

Heat the barbeque or grill to high. Drain the apricots well. Lift the lamb from the marinade, brush off and reserve any excess marinade. Thread the meat onto 4 long skewers, alternating every couple of pieces with onion wedges and apricots. Cook for 10 minutes, turning regularly and brushing with the reserved marinade until charred in places and cooked through. Serve immediately.

# STEAK

# CHIMICHURRI

Chimichurri apparently translates as a mix of ingredients, added in no particular order, and that's how you should approach this sharp, herby sauce. Use any herbs you may have spare and spoon generously over the charred meat.

 SERVES 2

 TAKES 20 minutes

large handful flat-leaf parsley, roughly chopped
2 tbsp oregano leaves
1 tbsp thyme leaves
1 red chilli, deseeded and finely chopped
2 garlic cloves, crushed
2 tbsp red wine vinegar
3 tbsp olive oil, plus a drizzle
knob of butter
400g/14oz onglet or hanger steak, trimmed of any sinew
200g/7oz cherry vine tomatoes
salt and freshly ground black pepper

**To serve**
2 flatbreads
salad

To make the chimichurri sauce, put the parsley, oregano, and thyme on a large chopping board and run a sharp knife through the herbs until they are finely chopped. Add the chilli and garlic with some seasoning. Scrape into a bowl and add the vinegar and oil. Cover and set aside.

Bring the steak to room temperature and rub it all over with a little oil. Heat a frying pan over a high heat, add the butter and when sizzling, add the steak and cook for 6–8 minutes, turning every couple of minutes and basting in the butter until brown all over. Remove from the heat, transfer the steak to a board, cover, and rest for 5 minutes.

Meanwhile, return the pan to the heat and tip in the tomatoes. Fry for 3 minutes, shaking the pan to ensure the tomatoes cook all over. Warm a couple of flatbreads, thinly slice the steak, then pile on top of the bread, spooning on the tomatoes and any resting juices from the meat. Finally, dollop some chimichurri sauce on top before eating. Any leftover chimichurri can be stored in the fridge for up to a week.

# PIQUILLO PEPPER &

★

# CHORIZO SKEWERS

---

Don't waste any of those vibrant red oils from your charred chorizo; instead, let the hot oil soak into your tomato bread for a true Spanish flavour. Great as a tapa with a glass of sherry.

 SERVES 4

 TAKES 10 minutes

190g/6½oz cooking chorizo
    sausages (about 12 mini chorizo)
12 piquillo peppers from a jar,
    drained
**For the tomato bread**
2 rustic demi-baguettes, halved
    lengthways
4 medium tomatoes, finely
    chopped
1 garlic clove, finely chopped
2 tbsp olive oil
½ tsp red wine vinegar
handful flat-leaf parsley, roughly
    chopped
salt and freshly ground black
    pepper

Halve the chorizo sausages lengthways, then thread the chorizo and peppers onto 4 small skewers, alternating between the two. Set aside.

Heat a griddle pan to high and cook the skewers for 5 minutes, turning halfway through until the chorizo is cooked through and has released its red oil. Remove the skewers from the pan and set aside. Lay the baguette halves cut-side down on the pan, moving them about in the hot oil, and toast for 2 minutes until a little crisp and red from the chorizo oil.

Combine the tomatoes, garlic, olive oil, vinegar, and parsley. Season with black pepper and a little salt, though the chorizo may be salty enough. Put the baguettes onto a serving plate, spoon over the tomatoes, and serve the skewers on top of the bread.

# BLACKBERRY & CHILLI
★
# PEPPERED VENISON

Venison is a dark, rich, and lean meat, delicious coated in punchy peppercorns and served with this sweet, sticky sauce with a chilli kick. A simple, sophisticated meal when accompanied by mashed potatoes.

 SERVES 2

 TAKES 25 minutes

300g/10oz venison loin steaks, cut into 2.5cm/1in cubes
2 tbsp black peppercorns
1 tbsp plain (all-purpose) flour
1 tbsp light-flavoured oil (such as vegetable oil)
salt and freshly ground black pepper
**For the blackberry and chilli sauce**
1 tbsp light-flavoured oil (such as vegetable oil)
knob of butter
2 shallots, finely chopped
1 garlic clove, crushed
1 red chilli, deseeded and finely chopped
150g/5½oz blackberries
2 tbsp caster sugar
mashed potato, to serve

Thread the venison onto 4 small skewers. Crush the peppercorns in a pestle and mortar, then tip out onto a plate and stir in the flour, adding a good pinch of salt. Turn the skewers in the peppercorn mix, gently pressing the mixture onto the meat so that it sticks. Set aside.

Meanwhile, make the blackberry and chilli sauce. Heat the oil and butter in a small frying pan. When foaming, add the shallots and cook for 5 minutes until soft and light golden. Add the garlic and chilli and cook for a further minute. Tip in the blackberries and sugar and cook for 3–5 minutes until the blackberries are beginning to break down – you want some to remain unpopped. Season and remove from the heat.

Place a large frying pan over a medium–high heat. Tip in the oil, swirl to coat the pan, then cook the venison skewers for 6 minutes, turning every couple of minutes, until crisp on the outside and golden. Remove from the heat and transfer to a plate to rest.

Serve the venison skewers with mashed potato, adding any resting juices to the blackberry sauce, and serve spooned over the skewers.

# KOHLRABI SLAW &
## ★
# SPICED LAMB CHOPS

Chops are such a huge kebab tradition. You can use your
chop as a scoop to pile all that slaw into your mouth
without any cutlery at all! The yogurt in the marinade
makes the meat meltingly tender.

 SERVES 4

 TAKES 30 minutes,
plus marinating

5 tbsp Greek yogurt
3 garlic cloves, crushed
2 tsp ground cumin
2 tsp ground coriander
½ tsp turmeric
½ tsp chilli flakes
1 tsp dried mint
12 lamb chop cutlets
salt and freshly ground black
    pepper
**For the kohlrabi slaw**
1 kohlrabi
½ sweetheart cabbage
2 tbsp mayonnaise
2 tbsp Greek yogurt
2 tsp Dijon mustard
handful coriander (cilantro)
handful mint
4 lavash or flatbreads, to serve

In a large bowl mix the yogurt, garlic, dried
spices, and herbs with plenty of seasoning. Stir to
combine, then tip in the chops and toss to coat in
the marinade, making sure the meat is covered in
yogurt. Cover, chill and set aside for at least 1 hour;
if you have time, the chops will sit happily for up to
24 hours.

To make the slaw, snip any leaves off the
kohlrabi. Peel it, cut into discs, then thinly slice
into matchsticks, and transfer to a large bowl.
Shred the cabbage and add it to the bowl. Mix
the mayonnaise, yogurt, and mustard with some
seasoning, then mix into the slaw and set aside.

Bring the chops to room temperature about 30
minutes before you are going to cook them. Heat
a barbeque or griddle pan to high and cook the
chops for 6–8 minutes, turning halfway through.
Allow the chops to rest for 2 minutes on top of the
flatbreads (warmed in the oven) you'll be serving.

Roughly chop the fresh herbs and fold through the
slaw before serving with the kebabs.

# PINEAPPLE SALSA &
★
# ROAST PORK BELLY

Dreamily tender pork, here combined with sweet and sour salsa, and salty, crisp skin sprinkled over for an explosion of taste and texture.

 SERVES 4-6

TAKES 3½ hours

2kg/4lb 8oz pork belly, skin scored (get your butcher to do this)
1 tbsp olive oil
1 tbsp soft brown sugar
1 tbsp smoked paprika
½ tsp chilli powder
zest and juice 1 orange (retain the orange halves)
salt

**For the pineapple salsa**
1 pineapple, peeled and cut into slices
1 red onion, finely chopped
1–2 red chillies, deseeded and finely chopped
bunch coriander (cilantro), finely chopped
juice 1 lime

**To serve**
corn tortillas
soured cream

Preheat the oven to 220°C/200°C fan/gas 7. Put the pork in a deep roasting dish. Mix the oil, sugar, paprika, and chilli powder with the orange zest to a paste, then rub all over the pork, making sure you work it into the skin. Season generously with salt, then roast for 30 minutes.

Reduce the oven temperature to 160°C/140°C fan/gas 3. Add the orange juice and squeezed oranges to the dish, along with 100ml/3½fl oz/scant ½ cup cold water, cover with foil, then return to the oven for 2½ hours. Check halfway through cooking and top up with water if the pan is drying out.

Meanwhile, make the pineapple salsa. Heat a griddle pan to high and cook the pineapple slices for 1–2 minutes on each side until charred in places. Remove and roughly chop, then allow to cool before mixing with the onion, chillies, coriander, and lime juice. Set aside.

Remove the pork crackling from the top of the belly joint using a sharp knife. If the crackling is not very crisp flash it under a hot grill until bubbled up and crisp – keep watching all the time.

Slice the pork and pile onto warmed corn tortillas with the salsa and a dollop of soured cream. Sprinkle crispy crackling all over the top, roll up, and eat.

POULTRY

★

# KEBABS

# LEMONGRASS
★
# CHICKEN & SPRING ONIONS

---

Delicately flavoured skewers that need nothing more than
a bowl of boiled rice for the perfect meal.

 SERVES 2

 TAKES 15 minutes,
plus marinating

1 lemongrass stalk, tough outer
   leaves removed
1 red chilli, deseeded and finely
   chopped
2 tbsp dark soy sauce
1 tbsp rice wine vinegar
1 tbsp clear honey
1 tsp sesame oil, plus a little for
   greasing
4 boneless, skinless chicken
   thighs, cut into 2.5cm/1in cubes
6 spring onions (scallions), cut into
   2.5cm/1in lengths

Bash the lemongrass with the back of a knife until
it really starts to break up, then finely chop with a
sharp knife. Scrape into a medium bowl and add
the chilli, soy sauce, vinegar, honey, and oil. Add the
chicken and stir to coat in the marinade. Cover and
leave to stand for 10 minutes.

Preheat the grill to high. Lightly grease a baking
sheet. Lift the chicken from the marinade and
thread it and the spring onions onto 4 small
skewers, alternating between the two. Transfer to
the baking sheet, pour over any excess marinade
and grill for 8–10 minutes, turning regularly until
charred in places and cooked through.

# BAHARAT

# CHICKEN WITH LABNEH

This kebab is a perfect balance of flavours; juicy aromatic spiced chicken, garlicky, creamy labneh, and crispy fried savoury onions, all topped off with little pops of sweet and sour pomegranate.

SERVES 2

TAKES 25 minutes, plus straining

4 skin-on boneless chicken thighs
2 tbsp baharat spice mix
½ tsp ground cinnamon
2 shallots, thinly sliced
1 tbsp plain (all-purpose) flour
3 tbsp olive oil
salt and freshly ground black
     pepper
**For the labneh**
200g/7oz Greek yogurt
1 garlic clove, crushed
handful flat-leaf parsley, finely
     chopped
½ tsp salt
**To serve**
1 baby gem lettuce, torn
50g/1¾oz pomegranate seeds
2 flatbreads

Start by making the labneh. Set a sieve over a large bowl and line it with a couple of sheets of kitchen paper. Mix the yogurt, garlic, parsley, and salt together, then spoon the mixture into the centre of the sieve. Gather up the corners of the kitchen paper and secure. Leave to strain for at least 30 minutes.

Meanwhile, rub the chicken with the baharat and cinnamon, and season well. Set aside.

Toss the shallots in the flour. Heat the oil in a large frying pan over a medium–high heat and cook the shallots until golden and crisp – about 5 minutes. Remove with a slotted spoon and drain on kitchen paper. You may have to do this in batches as the shallots burn easily and colour quickly.

Heat a barbeque or griddle pan to high. Cook the chicken, skin-side down, for 5 minutes. Flip over and cook for a further 3 minutes until cooked through and charred in places. Allow to rest for 5 minutes.

Unwrap the herby labneh, thickly slice the chicken thighs, and serve with lettuce and the pomegranate seeds in a warm flatbread.

# SPICY CORIANDER
★
# CHICKEN KOFTAS

---

Jam-packed with flavour, this is a really good low-fat kebab
option if you are being healthy but still fancy a tasty treat.

 SERVES 4

 TAKES 20 minutes

500g/1lb 2oz chicken mince
large bunch coriander (cilantro),
   finely chopped
2 green chillies, deseeded and
   finely chopped
1 garlic clove, crushed
1 tsp ground cumin
1 tsp ground coriander
¼ tsp ground turmeric
vegetable oil, for greasing
1 red onion, thinly sliced
juice ½ lemon
salt and freshly ground black
   pepper
**To serve**
4 flatbreads
salad
½ lemon, cut into wedges

Put the chicken mince into a large bowl and add
most of the chopped coriander, reserving a little
for garnish. Add the chillies, garlic, and spices with
plenty of seasoning. Massage with your hands for
2 minutes – this will combine the ingredients and
help the kebabs stay together as they cook.

Heat the grill or barbeque to high. Divide the
chicken mixture into 4 equal portions. With
damp hands, squeeze the meat onto 4 thick, long
skewers. Grease a baking sheet with a little oil and
lay the kofta in a single layer. Cook the kofta for 8
minutes, turning halfway through, until golden and
cooked through.

While the chicken is cooking, mix the onion with
the lemon juice in a small bowl and set aside. Serve
the hot chicken kebabs rolled in a flatbread with
the pickled onion, salad, and lemon wedges on
the side.

# STICKY CHINESE

★

# FIVE-SPICE DUCK

Serve this as a main meal with rice and stir-fried greens,
or thread the duck onto little skewers and serve with
drinks – perfect with a lychee Martini.

 SERVES 2

 TAKES 20 minutes,
plus marinating

2 tbsp dark soy sauce
1 tbsp clear honey
3cm/1in piece ginger, peeled and
   grated
1 garlic clove, crushed
1 tsp five-spice powder
¼ tsp hot chilli powder
2 skinless duck breasts, cut into
   2cm/1in cubes
**For the cucumber noodles**
½ cucumber
1 carrot
2 spring onions (scallions),
   shredded
1 tbsp dark soy sauce
3cm/1in piece ginger, peeled and
   finely grated
2 tsp sesame oil
1 tbsp toasted sesame seeds

Mix the soy sauce along with the honey, ginger,
garlic, and spices in a medium bowl. Add the duck,
gently coat in the marinade, then cover and leave
to stand for 15 minutes.

To make the cucumber noodles, halve the
cucumber lengthways and scoop out the seeds
using a teaspoon and discard. Cut the cucumber
into long, thin strips using a julienne peeler – if you
don't have one a potato peeler will do the trick.
Do the same with the carrot. Put the cucumber and
carrot strips into a bowl with the spring onions. Mix
the soy sauce, ginger, and oil, then pour over the
vegetables. Scatter over most of the sesame seeds
and set aside.

Preheat the grill to high. Lift the duck out of the
marinade and thread onto 4 small skewers. Cook
for 6 minutes, brushing with extra marinade halfway
through cooking and just before turning. The
duck should be dark golden, sticky, cooked on the
outside, and a little pink in the centre. Leave to rest
for a few minutes.

Serve the skewers with the cucumber noodles
sprinkled with the remaining sesame seeds and any
resting juices.

# PRESERVED LEMON
★
# CHICKEN WITH ZA'ATAR

Chicken thighs are the chef's choice for good reason. The mixture of dark and white meat, and the fatty skin help to keep the meat juicy and packed with flavour.

 SERVES 4

 TAKES 20 minutes, plus marinating

2 tbsp za'atar
2 garlic cloves, crushed
1 tbsp olive oil, plus a drizzle
1 tsp sumac
juice ½ lemon
8 boneless, skin-on chicken thighs
**For the preserved lemon yogurt sauce**
1 preserved lemon, plus 2 tbsp juice from the jar
200g/7oz natural yogurt
2 tbsp tahini
salt and freshly ground black pepper
**To serve**
4 flatbreads
large handful flat-leaf parsley, roughly chopped
½ red onion, thinly sliced
½ lemon, cut into wedges

In a large bowl mix the za'atar, garlic, oil, sumac, and lemon juice. Add the chicken and toss to coat. Cover and leave to marinate for 15 minutes.

To make the sauce, quarter the preserved lemon, scoop out and discard the flesh, then finely chop the skin. Mix this with the yogurt and tahini, then add the preserving juice from the jar, taste, and season. If necessary, add a couple of tablespoons cold water to loosen the sauce. Set aside.

Heat a barbeque or griddle pan to high. Lift the chicken thighs out of the marinade and shake off any excess juices. Cook skin-side down for 5 minutes, then flip over and cook for a further 5 minutes until cooked right through. Remove from the heat and allow to rest for a couple of minutes.

Serve the kebabs with flatbreads, the preserved lemon sauce, the parsley, onion, and lemon wedges.

# DUCK SATAY

★

# SKEWERS

Duck is a dark and deeply flavoured meat that works so well with spicy peanut satay sauce. You can use crunchy or smooth peanut butter, depending on your preference.

 SERVES 4

 TAKES 20 minutes, plus marinating

4 tbsp crunchy peanut butter
3cm/1in piece ginger, peeled and grated
2 tbsp dark soy sauce
2 limes
1 Thai red chilli, deseeded and finely chopped
1 tsp ground turmeric
½ tsp ground cumin
½ tsp ground coriander
½ tsp caster sugar
4 skinless duck breasts
1 tbsp red curry paste
200ml/7fl oz coconut milk
½ cucumber, cut into batons
1 red onion, thinly sliced
handful salted peanuts, roughly chopped
handful coriander (cilantro), roughly chopped
handful mint, roughly chopped
salt and freshly ground black pepper
boiled white rice, to serve

Put the peanut butter, ginger, soy sauce, juice of 1 lime, chilli, and spices into a bowl. Add the sugar and some seasoning, then stir to combine. Cut the duck breasts into long strips, add to the bowl and toss to coat, cover, and leave to stand for 30 minutes.

Preheat the grill to high. Thread the duck onto 8–12 small skewers, pushing any excess marinade back into the bowl – keep this for later. Put the skewers onto a baking sheet and grill for 12 minutes, turning every couple of minutes, until charred in places and cooked through.

Meanwhile, heat the curry paste in a small pan until fragrant. Scrape in the reserved marinade and fry for 1 minute, stirring continuously. Pour in the coconut milk and stir to combine. Heat the sauce, but do not allow it to boil. Remove the pan from the heat.

Serve the skewers with the sauce poured over, alongside the cucumber and onion scattered with the peanuts, herbs, and boiled rice. Chop the remaining lime into wedges for squeezing.

# CHICKEN LIVER
★
# EN BROCHETTE

Chicken liver skewers are enjoyed all over North Africa, lightly spiced and stuffed between a couple of slices of bread with fresh salad and plenty of herbs. Chicken livers are milder in flavour than other offal, and economical too.

 SERVES 4

 TAKES 30 minutes

300g/10oz chicken livers, trimmed
1 tsp ground cumin
1 tsp ground coriander
½ tsp ground cinnamon
1 tbsp olive oil
50g/1¾oz butter
1 tsp soft brown sugar
25ml/scant 1fl oz Marsala
4 slices sourdough bread
handful flat-leaf parsley, roughly
    chopped
salt and freshly ground black
    pepper

Thread the chicken livers onto 4 small skewers. Lay the skewers on a baking tray and dust them with the cumin, coriander, and cinnamon. Season and set aside.

Heat a large frying pan over a high heat, then add the oil and a knob of the butter. Once foaming, cook the skewers for 5 minutes, turning halfway through, until golden and cooked through – you may have to do this in batches. Sprinkle the sugar over the skewers and pour in the Marsala with plenty of seasoning. Shake the pan to remove any sediment from the bottom of the pan, then remove from the heat.

Toast the sourdough, spread the remaining butter over each slice, and serve the skewers on top. Pour over the pan juices and sprinkle with the parsley.

# KOREAN

★

# CHICKEN SKEWERS

Gochujang sauce is a fermented sauce made from, amongst other things, red chilli and fermented soya beans. Spicy, salty, and addictive, it can be found in Asian supermarkets and in some supermarkets. Use it sparingly!

 SERVES 4

 TAKES 20 minutes, plus marinating

5cm/2in piece ginger, peeled and grated
2 garlic cloves, crushed
3 tbsp dark soy sauce
2 tbsp gochujang sauce
2 tbsp rice wine vinegar
1 tbsp clear honey
1 tsp sesame oil
8 boneless, skinless chicken thighs, cut into 2.5cm/1in cubes

**To serve**
1 tbsp toasted sesame seeds
4 spring onions (scallions), shredded
boiled white rice
kimchi

In a large bowl mix the ginger, garlic, soy sauce, gochujang, vinegar, honey, and oil. Stir to combine, then add the chicken and toss to coat in the sauce. Cover, chill and leave to marinate for 30 minutes.

Preheat the grill to high. Thread the chicken onto 8–12 small skewers. Lay the skewers on a baking sheet and grill for 12 minutes, turning a couple of times during cooking, until the chicken is charred in places and cooked through. Sprinkle with the sesame seeds and scatter with the spring onions. Serve with boiled rice and some kimchi.

# SPICED

★

# SPATCHCOCK POUSSINS

Poussins not only look great but taste great too. When you want a change from chicken, these little birds are just the thing. Serve one per person, doused in sticky pomegranate molasses; they really are finger-licking good.

 SERVES 2

 TAKES 30 minutes

2 poussins
1 tbsp olive oil, plus a drizzle
1 tsp ground cinnamon
1 tsp ground cumin
1 tsp dried thyme
¼ tsp chilli powder
pinch allspice
3 tbsp pomegranate molasses
salt and freshly ground black
    pepper
**For the walnut salad**
50g/1¾oz toasted walnuts
large handful flat-leaf parsley,
    finely chopped
large handful mint, finely chopped
½ red onion, very finely chopped
100g/3½oz pomegranate seeds
juice ½ lemon
flatbreads, to serve

First spatchcock the poussins: place the birds on a chopping board, breast-side down. Take a pair of kitchen scissors and cut along one side of the back bone, repeat on the other side, then lift out and discard the backbone. Flip the poussins over and, one at a time, flatten the breast with the palm of your hand so that the birds lie flat. Skewer the birds with 2 skewers inserted diagonally to form a criss-cross. Drizzle each bird with the oil. Mix the cinnamon, cumin, thyme, chilli powder, allspice, and seasoning together, then rub all over the birds.

Heat a barbeque or griddle pan to high. Cook the birds for 18 minutes, weighing them down with a heavy pan so that the birds are in complete contact with the heat. Turn the poussins halfway through the cook time and cook until charred in places and cooked through. Remove from the heat, transfer to a plate, and drizzle over 2 tablespoons of the pomegranate molasses. Cover and leave to rest.

Next, make the walnut salad. Finely chop the walnuts and tip them into a bowl. Add the parsley, mint, onion, and pomegranate seeds. Pour over the remaining pomegranate molasses, the lemon juice, and a drizzle of oil. Serve the poussins with the salad and flatbreads

# SPICED

# CHICKEN & BABA GANOUSH

This smoky baba ganoush enriched with luxurious tahini
will work just as well with roast squash or fried halloumi.

  SERVES 4

TAKES 1 hour

2 medium aubergines (eggplants),
    pricked all over with a fork
olive oil, for rubbing
2 green (bell) peppers
4 mild green chillies
200g/7oz Greek yogurt
2 tbsp tahini
1 garlic clove, crushed
juice 1 lemon
2 large tomatoes, deseeded and
    roughly chopped
handful coriander (cilantro),
    roughly chopped
6 skin-on boneless chicken thighs
1 tbsp ground cumin
1 tbsp smoked paprika
salt and freshly ground black
    pepper
4 flatbreads, to serve

Heat a barbeque or grill to high. Put the aubergines
on a baking tray and rub with a little oil. Cook for 25
minutes, but after 10 minutes add the green peppers
and chillies to the tray. Cook until charred – keep
watching as you just want them to blacken and soften
but not to dry out. Transfer the peppers and chillies to
a bowl and cover with clingfilm (plastic wrap). When
the aubergines are charred, and soft when a skewer
is inserted, remove from the heat and allow to cool.
Halve the aubergines lengthways and scrape out the
flesh using a spoon. Discard the skin. Tip the flesh into
a food processor, then add the yogurt, tahini, garlic,
and half the lemon juice. Whizz until smooth, season,
and set aside.

Remove and discard the charred skins from the
peppers and chillies, then finely chop the flesh and
add to a bowl with the tomatoes, coriander, and the
remaining lemon juice. Set aside.

Heat a griddle pan to hot, dust the chicken thighs with
the cumin and paprika, then cook skin-side down for 5
minutes. Flip over and cook for a further 3–5 minutes
until cooked through. Remove from the pan and allow
to rest for a few minutes.

Warm the flatbreads in a hot oven, spread with the
baba ganoush, sprinkle over the salsa, and top with
thick slices of charred chicken.

# HERBY

# CHICKEN WINGS

Threading chicken wings onto skewers is done throughout
the Middle East and Turkey where kebabs are cooked
over huge coal pits. It helps to stop the wings falling
through into the hot embers, but the metal skewers help
to cook the meat from the inside while the hot coals do
the work on the outside.

 SERVES 4

 TAKES 30 minutes,
plus marinating

200g/7oz natural yogurt
3 garlic cloves, crushed
handful coriander (cilantro),
   finely chopped
handful flat-leaf parsley, finely
   chopped
1 tbsp thyme leaves
1 tsp ground cumin
1 tsp hot chilli powder
3 tbsp clear honey
16 chicken wings, tips removed
salt and freshly ground black
   pepper
**To serve**
4–8 flatbreads
sweet chilli sauce

In a large bowl, mix the yogurt, garlic, herbs,
spices, and honey. Set aside.

Halve the chicken wings through the joint, drop
these into the marinade, toss to coat, season, then
cover and chill for at least 30 minutes or up to 24
hours if you have time.

Heat a barbeque or grill to high. Thread the
chicken wings onto 4 long or 8 smaller skewers.
Cook for 18 minutes, turning every couple of
minutes, until the chicken wings are charred on
the outside and cooked through – you may have
to remove a wing to unveil the inside to check if
the meat is cooked.

Serve with flatbreads and sweet chilli sauce
for dipping.

CHERMOULA MAYO

★

# CHICKEN & ORANGE SALAD

Fennel, orange, and chicken make such a refreshing combination. Together they look and taste so good. Definitely one to serve to your poshest pals.

 SERVES 4

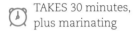 TAKES 30 minutes, plus marinating

1 tbsp fennel seeds
1 tsp chilli flakes
2 oranges
1 head of fennel, shaved with a mandoline, fronds reserved
6 skin-on boneless chicken thighs

**For the chermoula mayo**
handful coriander (cilantro)
handful flat-leaf parsley
½ preserved lemon, rind only
1 garlic clove
1 tsp smoked paprika
1 tsp ground cumin
6 tbsp mayonnaise
salt and freshly ground black pepper
4 flatbreads, to serve

Heat the fennel seeds in a dry frying pan for 1–2 minutes, or until fragrant. Tip them into a pestle and mortar, add the chilli flakes and a good pinch of salt, and grind to a rough powder. Add the zest of the oranges and the juice of half of one orange, and mix well. Put the chicken in a baking dish, pour over the marinade, rub in, then leave to stand for at least 30 minutes.

Meanwhile, make the chermoula mayo. Put the coriander, parsley, preserved lemon rind, and garlic onto a chopping board and run a sharp knife over until everything is finely chopped. Scrape up into a bowl and add the paprika, cumin, mayonnaise, and 1 tablespoon of the liquid from the preserved lemon jar, then season and set aside.

Peel the remaining oranges and finely chop the flesh, then toss with the fennel and set aside.

Heat a barbeque or griddle pan to high. Cook the chicken skin-side down for 5 minutes, then flip over and cook for a further 3 minutes, or until cooked through. Transfer to a chopping board and slice.

Heat the flatbreads, pile on the fennel and orange, chicken, and a dollop of chermoula mayo.

# TURKEY

★

# SHISH

The secret to keeping these kebabs juicy is to use thin slices of turkey and to pack them tightly onto skewers, like a big turkey doner kebab. The marinade keeps the centre of the meat moist while the outside is beautifully charred.

 SERVES 4

 TAKES 20 minutes, plus marinating

800g/1lb 12oz turkey breast steaks
6 tbsp Greek yogurt
3 garlic cloves, crushed
small handful flat-leaf parsley, finely chopped
2 tsp dried oregano
1 tsp ground cumin
½ tsp chilli flakes
2 onions, cut into eighths
salt and freshly ground black pepper

**To serve**
1 lemon, cut into wedges
salad (shredded cabbage, tomatoes, and cucumber)
4 flatbreads

Put the turkey breasts between two sheets of clingfilm (plastic wrap) on a chopping board and flatten with a rolling pin until about 5mm/¼in thick. Discard the clingfilm, then chop the turkey into 3cm/1in cubes. Set aside.

Mix the yogurt, garlic, most of the parsley, oregano, cumin, and chilli flakes with plenty of seasoning. Add the turkey and toss to combine, making sure all the meat is coated in the marinade. Leave to stand for 15 minutes.

Heat a barbeque or grill to high. Thread the turkey onto 4 long skewers, alternating with chunks of onion. Lay the skewers on a baking sheet and cook for 12 minutes, turning a couple of times, until charred in parts and cooked through. Scatter with the parsley and serve with the lemon wedges, salad and flatbreads.

# FISH & SEAFOOD

★

# KEBABS

# SESAME-CRUSTED

★

# TUNA WITH WASABI MAYO

Light and fresh, this is one of those recipes that you will revisit time and again. Perfect for lunch or a speedy supper.

 SERVES 2

 TAKES 15 minutes, plus marinating

4 tbsp dark soy sauce
4 tbsp mirin
½ tsp soft brown sugar
250g/9oz tuna steak, cut into
　2cm/1in cubes
3 tbsp sesame seeds (black, white,
　or mixed)
3 tbsp mayonnaise
1 tsp wasabi
200g/7oz buckwheat noodles
100g/3½oz frozen edamame beans
1 tsp sesame oil
pickled ginger, to serve

In a medium bowl, mix 2 tablespoons each of soy sauce and mirin with the sugar. Add the tuna and carefully toss to coat in the sauce, then cover and chill for 1 hour.

Sprinkle the sesame seeds onto a plate. Lift the tuna out of the marinade and shake off any excess juices. Drain on kitchen paper, then thread onto 4 small wooden skewers. Roll the skewers in the sesame seeds, pressing them on if necessary. Set aside.

Mix the mayonnaise and wasabi together in a small bowl, then set aside. Cook the noodles in a pan of boiling salted water according to packet instructions. Add the edamame beans 3 minutes before the end of cooking. Drain well, run the noodles and beans under cold water to cool, drain again, then place in a bowl and pour over the sesame oil, remaining soy sauce and mirin.

Heat a large non-stick frying pan to high and cook the tuna skewers for 30 seconds on each side. The tuna will be rare, so increase the cooking time if you prefer it well cooked. Divide the noodles between bowls, serve with the skewers, pickled ginger, and wasabi mayo for dipping.

# GARLIC & LEMON

★

# COD & PEACH SKEWERS

These can be thrown together in a matter of moments, perfect for a last-minute summer supper, when all the ingredients are at their best. You want the thick end of the cod fillet as this will hold together better during cooking.

 SERVES 2

 TAKES 15 minutes

2 tbsp olive oil
2 tbsp thyme leaves
3 garlic cloves, finely chopped
zest 1 lemon
300g/10oz cod fillet, cut into
　3cm/1in cubes
2 firm, ripe peaches, cut into
　quarters
salt and freshly ground black
　pepper
**To serve**
lemon wedges
green salad

Heat a grill or barbeque to high. In a large bowl, mix the oil, thyme, and garlic with the lemon zest and plenty of seasoning. Add the cod and peaches, and very carefully toss to coat.

Thread the cod and peaches onto 4 skewers, alternating between the two. Brush over any excess marinade, then cook for 6–8 minutes, turning halfway through and brushing with more marinade, until the cod is cooked through and the peaches are golden. Squeeze over the lemon wedges. Serve immediately with a big green salad.

# HARISSA

# SARDINES

It is worth spending a bit of money on good harissa; a little jar will go a long way and just a small amount can add spice and a delicious flavour to a variety of fish and meat.

**SERVES 4**

**TAKES** 45 minutes, plus marinating

400g/14oz can chickpeas
  (garbanzo beans), drained
  and rinsed
1 tbsp olive oil
½ tsp ground cumin
½ tsp smoked paprika
¼ tsp ground cinnamon
salt and freshly ground black
  pepper
**For the sardines**
2 tbsp rose harissa paste
zest and juice ½ lemon
bunch coriander (cilantro), leaves
  and stems separated
8–12 fresh sardines, gutted
**To serve**
200g/7oz Greek yogurt
1 garlic clove, crushed
4 flatbreads
½ lemon, cut into wedges

Preheat the oven to 200°C/180°C fan/gas 6. Use a clean tea towel to dry the chickpeas really well. Tip the chickpeas onto a baking sheet with a lip, transfer to the oven, and bake for 5 minutes. Remove, drizzle with the oil, scatter over the spices and plenty of seasoning, and toss to coat. Return to the oven for 5 minutes, or until starting to crisp at the edges and turn golden.

Meanwhile, prepare the sardines. Mix the harissa paste with the lemon zest and juice in a small bowl. Finely chop the coriander stems and add them to the mix with plenty of seasoning. Insert a skewer into the tail end of each sardine, skewer through the cavity and out through the mouth of the fish. Rub all over with the harissa paste and leave to marinate for 10 minutes.

Meanwhile, mix the yogurt and garlic with some seasoning in a small bowl. Set aside. Heat a griddle pan or barbeque to high and cook the sardines for 3 minutes on each side.

Heat the flatbreads and spread with the garlic yogurt. Pile on the chickpeas and sardines, and scatter with the chopped coriander leaves. Serve with lemon wedges to squeeze over.

# ANCHOVY & TOMATO

★

# PAPRIKA FLATBREADS

Sweet, juicy tomatoes and salty anchovies are a match
made in heaven. Use ripe vine tomatoes for this dish –
you want them to pop and release their juices as you
bite into them.

 SERVES 2

 TAKES 15 minutes

200g/7oz small mixed vine-
   ripened tomatoes
1 tsp olive oil
25g/scant 1oz butter, softened
1 tsp smoked paprika
1 garlic clove, crushed
handful flat-leaf parsley, finely
   chopped
2 flatbreads, such as piadina
8 anchovies, halved lengthways

Heat a griddle pan to high. Drizzle the tomatoes
with the oil and cut a few in half. Put them on the
griddle pan and cook for 3–5 minutes until blistered
and juicy. Remove and set aside.

In a small bowl, mix the butter with the paprika,
garlic, and parsley. Set aside.

Cook the flatbreads on the griddle pan until hot
and beginning to take on some colour. Spread
with the paprika butter and top with the griddled
tomatoes, lay over the anchovies, and serve
immediately.

# CHARRED BABY GEM &
★
# KING PRAWN KEBAB

---

This is a posh prawn cocktail kebab – all the flavours but none of the naff. Leave the shells on to cook the prawns and peel them at the table before dropping the succulent meat, coated in chilli butter, onto your flatbread.

  SERVES 2

TAKES 20 minutes

25g/scant 1oz butter, softened
1 tbsp chipotle chilli paste
1 red chilli, deseeded and finely chopped
1 garlic clove, finely chopped
zest 1 lemon
1 tbsp chopped chives
2 baby gem lettuces, quartered lengthways
175g/6oz raw jumbo king prawns
100g/3½oz vine cherry tomatoes, roughly chopped
**To serve**
2 flatbreads
1 lemon, cut into wedges

In a small bowl, mix the butter, chilli paste and chilli, garlic, and lemon zest with most of the chives. Cover until required.

Heat a griddle pan to high. Add the lettuce, cut-side down, and cook for 2 minutes, flipping halfway through. Remove from the pan. Add the prawns to the pan and cook for 3–4 minutes, turning halfway until pink and cooked through. Turn off the heat, add the chilli and garlic butter to the pan, and shake to coat the prawns.

Warm the flatbreads, then pile them with the charred lettuce and buttery prawns, making sure you pour over all the pan juices, and the tomatoes. Finish with the reserved chives and serve with lemon wedges on the side.

# YUZU, SOY & HONEY
★
# SALMON SKEWERS

Yuzu juice is available in many supermarkets and specialist Asian stores. If you can't find it, replace it with a squeeze of any other citrus fruit; lemon or grapefruit works well.

 SERVES 4

 TAKES 15 minutes, plus marinating

2 tbsp dark soy sauce
2 tbsp yuzu juice
2 tbsp clear honey
1 tbsp sesame oil, plus a drizzle
3 garlic cloves, roughly chopped
4 skin-on salmon fillets (about 120g/4oz each), cut into 3cm/1in cubes
200g/7oz tenderstem broccoli
3cm/1in piece ginger, peeled and shredded
1 red chilli, deseeded and sliced
3 spring onions (scallions), shredded

In a medium bowl, mix the soy sauce, yuzu juice, honey, half the sesame oil and 1 garlic clove. Put the salmon pieces into the marinade, cover, and chill for 30 minutes.

Cook the broccoli in a pan of salted boiling water for 3 minutes, drain, and plunge into a bowl of ice-cold water to stop the cooking process. Drain again and set aside.

Lift the salmon pieces from the marinade, shake off any excess marinade, and reserve in the bowl. Thread the chunks onto 8 small skewers. Heat a frying pan over a high heat, add a drizzle of sesame oil, then cook the skewers, skin-side down, for 2 minutes, then flip over and cook for a further 3 minutes, turning every minute to brown all the sides. The salmon skin should be crispy and the flesh inside a little pink. If you like your salmon well done cook it for a further 1–2 minutes. Remove from the heat and keep warm.

Heat the remaining sesame oil in a pan, throw in the remaining garlic, the ginger, and chilli and stir-fry for 1 minute, then add the broccoli and toss to combine. Pour in the reserved marinade and bubble for 1 minute. Serve the salmon skewers on top of the broccoli, scattered with the spring onions.

Fish & Seafood Kebabs

# SUMAC & LEMON

★

# MACKEREL

This is a combination of two great Istanbul offerings: the mackerel sandwiches sold along the Bosphorus, and the kebabs sold all over the city. Sumac is a slightly sour berry that works well with the rich, oily mackerel.

 SERVES 2

 TAKES 15 minutes

2 boneless, skin-on mackerel fillets
1 tsp sumac, plus extra for
    sprinkling
½ tsp ground cumin
zest 1 lemon
1 dill pickle, finely chopped
2 Lebanese cucumbers, thinly
    sliced
½ red onion, sliced
handful dill, roughly chopped
handful flat-leaf parsley, roughly
    chopped
**To serve**
2 pitta breads
1 large tomato, thiny sliced
natural yogurt
pickled chillies
lemon wedges

Preheat the grill to high. Lay the mackerel on a baking sheet and sprinkle with the sumac, cumin, and lemon zest. Grill skin-side up for 2 minutes until crisp and charred in places. Flip over and cook for a further minute. Remove from the grill.

Mix the dill pickle, cucumbers, and onion together, then fold in the dill and parsley with 1 tablespoon pickling juice from the pickle jar to make a salad.

Warm the pittas, split them, and fill with a mackerel fillet, some salad, and tomato slices, and top with a dollop of yogurt. Serve sprinkled with extra sumac and pickled chillies, with lemon wedges on the side.

# AVOCADO &

★

# SEA BASS CEVICHE

The key to great ceviche is fresh fish. You can use any white fish for this, but the delicate taste and texture of sea bass is just perfect. Serve on griddled tacos for a little crunch alongside the silky-soft ceviche.

SERVES 2

TAKES 15 minutes

1 large firm ripe avocado, halved, peeled and pitted
1 red (bell) pepper, cut into thin strips
2 skinless, boneless sea bass fillets
juice 2 limes
½ small red onion, thinly sliced
1 red chilli, deseeded and finely chopped
corn tortillas
handful micro coriander (cilantro), to serve
olive oil, for drizzling

Heat a griddle pan to high. Cut the avocado into 6 wedges, then cook on the hot griddle pan with the red pepper for 2–3 minutes, gently turning halfway through, until both are charred in places. Remove and set aside.

Thinly slice the sea bass fillets and transfer to a small bowl. Add the lime juice, onion, and chilli, then toss to combine and leave to stand for 3 minutes.

Put the griddle pan back on the heat and cook the corn tortillas for 1 minute until just warmed. Transfer to a serving dish, pile on the charred avocado and red pepper, and spoon over the ceviche. Scatter with the micro coriander and drizzle with a little oil before eating.

# TANDOORI

★

# SALMON

Sometimes it's great to be given permission to cheat; do just that and buy a good-quality tandoori paste. It will capture all the flavours of a decent Indian takeaway in a jar, meaning you can whip up a delicious dinner in minutes.

 SERVES 4

 TAKES 15 minutes

2 tbsp tandoori paste
1 tbsp Greek yogurt
1 tsp light-flavoured oil (such as vegetable oil)
1 tsp ground coriander
4 x 120g/4oz skin-on salmon fillets
2 red onions, cut into wedges
**For the raita**
½ cucumber
handful mint, finely chopped
handful coriander (cilantro), finely chopped
½ garlic clove, crushed
½ tsp caster (superfine) sugar
200g/7oz Greek yogurt
1 lemon (½ juiced, ½ cut into wedges)
salt and freshly ground black pepper
**To serve**
4 chapattis
¼ iceberg lettuce, shredded
2 tomatoes, finely chopped

In a bowl, mix the tandoori paste, yogurt, oil, and ground coriander. Add the salmon and turn to coat in the marinade, then add the onions and coat with a little marinade, making sure most of it stays on the fish. Set aside.

To make the raita, halve the cucumber lengthways and use a teaspoon to scoop out and discard the seeds, then chop the remaining flesh. Put in a bowl, then stir in the mint, most of the coriander (reserving a little for garnish), the garlic, sugar, yogurt, and lemon juice. Season and set aside.

Preheat the grill to high. Put the salmon skin-side up on a baking sheet with the onions and grill for 4 minutes. Flip over and grill for a further 2 minutes, giving the onions a stir – remove any that are getting too charred; they should begin to soften but retain some crunch.

Heat the chapattis, flake the salmon over the bread, and serve with the onions, lettuce, tomatoes, a big dollop of raita, any reserved herbs, and a lemon wedge.

GARLIC & LEMON

★

# SQUID WITH CHORIZO

This is a version of Madrid's bocadillos stuffed with fried squid rings. Like the original, the best way to eat these skewers is fresh from the grill, piled into a crusty roll with lashings of paprika aïoli.

 SERVES 4

 TAKES 20 minutes, plus marinating

400g/14oz squid, cleaned (ask your fishmonger to do this)
1 lemon, zested
2 garlic cloves, roughly chopped
1 tbsp olive oil
150g/5½oz cooking chorizo, cut into 2.5cm/1in chunks
handful flat-leaf parsley, roughly chopped
salt and freshly ground black pepper
**For the aïoli**
6 tbsp mayonnaise
½ garlic clove, crushed
1 tbsp sweet smoked paprika
1 lemon, cut into wedges, to serve

Cut the squid into 2cm/1in rings and halve the tentacles. Transfer to a bowl and add the lemon zest, garlic, and oil. Season and set aside for 15 minutes.

Thread the squid onto 4 skewers, alternating with the chorizo, and brush with any marinade left in the bowl. Heat a barbeque or griddle pan to high and cook the skewers for 5 minutes, turning halfway through, until the squid and chorizo are charred in places and cooked through.

Meanwhile, make the aïoli. In a bowl, mix the mayonnaise, garlic, and paprika.

Scatter the skewers with the parsley and serve with the aïoli for dipping and the lemon cut into wedges for squeezing.

# SMOKED TROUT
★
# WITH DILL PICKLES

These dill pickles go brilliantly with all of the kebabs
in this book. Here they combine especially well with
smoked trout and a shallot yogurt to make a very special
breakfast, lunch, dinner or after-pub 'munch'.

 SERVES 4

 TAKES 45 minutes, plus
marinating

4 tbsp white wine vinegar
2 tbsp caster (superfine) sugar
1 star anise
1 tsp mustard seeds
handful dill sprigs
2 Lebanese cucumbers, sliced
knob of butter
1 tbsp olive oil
2 shallots, finely chopped
1 garlic clove, crushed
200g/7oz natural yogurt
4 wholemeal flatbreads
200g/7oz smoked trout
salt and freshly ground black
   pepper

Set a small pan over a medium heat and add the
vinegar, sugar, star anise, and mustard seeds along
with 1 tablespoon cold water and 4 dill sprigs.
Swirl the pan once the sugar has dissolved, then
remove from the heat and allow to cool. Add the
cucumbers and leave to stand for 30 minutes.

Heat the butter and oil in a frying pan. Once
foaming, add the shallots and plenty of seasoning,
then cook for about 5 minutes, stirring frequently
until soft and light golden. Add the garlic and cook
for a further minute. Remove from the heat and
scrape into a bowl, allowing the mixture to cool for
a few minutes before folding in the yogurt.

Heat the flatbreads in a warm oven, dollop on the
sweet shallot yogurt, pile on the smoked trout,
drain the pickled cucumbers, and serve on top of
the trout. Sprinkle with the remaining dill.

Fish & Seafood Kebabs

# TOASTED COCONUT

★

# MARINATED KING PRAWNS

You can find fresh curry leaves in Asian food shops and large supermarkets. Dried just don't have the same taste or distinctive exotic aroma. These skewers are lovely served with chapattis or a bowl of steamy cooked rice.

 SERVES 4

 TAKES 20 minutes, plus marinating

16 unpeeled raw jumbo king prawns
2 garlic cloves, crushed
3cm/1in piece ginger, peeled and grated
2 tsp garam masala
1 tsp ground turmeric
juice 1 lime, plus wedges to serve
1 tbsp light-flavoured oil (such as vegetable oil)
1 tsp black mustard seeds
2 tbsp (about 20) curry leaves
2 green finger chillies, finely sliced
3 tbsp desiccated coconut
handful coriander (cilantro), roughly chopped

Put the prawns into a large bowl and add the garlic, ginger, garam masala, turmeric, and lime juice. Use your hands to toss the prawns and coat in the marinade. Cover and leave to stand for 30 minutes.

Heat a barbeque or griddle pan to high. Thread the prawns onto 4 skewers, then cook for 4–5 minutes, turning halfway through, until pink and cooked.

Meanwhile, heat the oil in a frying pan. When hot, add the mustard seeds and curry leaves, and sizzle until fragrant, then add the chillies and fry for 1 minute. Reduce the heat and add the desiccated coconut, stirring continuously until light golden in colour. Remove from the heat and transfer to a bowl.

Serve the prawn skewers scattered with the toasted coconut mixture, sprinkle with the coriander, and squeeze over the juice from a lime wedge.

# LEMON

# MONKFISH SKEWERS

These sophisticated skewers are built from a handful
of fresh ingredients and a couple of dried spices.
They're quick and easy to assemble, but the taste
belies their simplicity.

 SERVES 4

 TAKES 20 minutes,
plus marinating

500g/1lb 2oz monkfish, cut into
   2.5cm/1in cubes
2 garlic cloves, finely chopped
1 red chilli, deseeded and finely
   chopped
1 tsp dried oregano
1 lemon
1 tbsp olive oil
salt and freshly ground black
   pepper
**To serve**
buttered basmati rice
kachumba salad (see page 24)
   (optional)

Put the monkfish into a large bowl with the garlic,
chilli, oregano, and plenty of seasoning. Cut the
lemon in half, juice and zest one half and pour over
the monkfish with the oil. Stir to combine. Cover
and leave to stand for 15 minutes.

Cut the remaining lemon half into small wedges,
then thread onto 4 large or 8 small skewers,
alternating with the monkfish.

Heat a barbeque or grill to high. Cook the skewers
for 6 minutes, turning halfway through and brushing
with any remaining marinade, until cooked through.

Serve with buttered basmati rice and katchumba
salad (if desired).

# VEGETARIAN

★

# KEBABS

# ROASTED BEETS &
★
# FRIED PANEER ON NAAN

Paneer takes on any flavours that you put with it. Here, mildly spiced with curry, it goes perfectly with the earthy beetroot and sweet mango chutney. You could thread the paneer onto skewers if you were having a barbeque.

 SERVES 4

 TAKES 45 minutes

8 small beetroots, scrubbed and quartered, and any small leaves reserved
2 tbsp olive oil
1 tsp cumin seeds
1 red onion, cut into wedges through the root
225g/8oz paneer
¼ tsp ground turmeric
3 tsp curry powder
4 small naan breads
4 tbsp Greek yogurt
4 tbsp mayonnaise
4 tbsp mango chutney
salt and freshly ground black pepper
**To serve**
handful chopped coriander (cilantro)
1 lime, cut into wedges

Preheat the oven to 200°C/180°C fan/gas 5. Put the beetroots on a baking tray and toss with 1 tablespoon of the oil and the cumin seeds. Roast for 40 minutes, but after 20 minutes, stir in the onion. You want the beets to be tender but still with a little bite.

Meanwhile, cut the paneer into 2cm/1in cubes and add to a bowl with the turmeric and 1 teaspoon of the curry powder, then stir to coat. Heat a frying pan, add the remaining oil and cook the paneer until golden and soft. Remove and toss with the roasted beets.

Heat the naan breads in a warm oven. Combine the yogurt, mayonnaise, and remaining curry powder in a small bowl. Season to taste. Top the warmed naans with a dollop of curry mayo, paneer, and beets. Drizzle with the mango chutney and a sprinkling of coriander, and any reserved beet leaves. Squeeze over the lime juice just before serving.

# GRIDDLED

# RED ONION WEDGES

These wedges are traditionally served in Turkish restaurants
at the start of a meal with a big plate of chopped salad.
They are great on their own with plenty of bread for
mopping up juices, or like this with feta and fattoush.

  SERVES 4

TAKES 15 minutes

6 red onions, each cut into 8
   wedges through the root
3 tbsp olive oil, plus a drizzle
2 tbsp pomegranate molasses
juice ½ lemon
1 garlic clove, crushed
1 tsp sumac
2 wholemeal flatbreads or pitta
   breads
large bunch flat-leaf parsley, finely
   chopped
2 large tomatoes, roughly chopped
100g/3½oz pomegranate seeds
100g/3½oz feta

Heat a grill or griddle pan to high. Thread the onion
wedges onto 2 large or 4 small skewers. Cook for
6–8 minutes, turning regularly until charred in
places and starting to soften. Remove from the
heat, slide the onion wedges off the skewers into a
bowl, pour over the oil, pomegranate molasses, and
lemon juice, then add the garlic and ½ teaspoon
sumac. Stir to combine and set aside.

Preheat the grill to high. Rip the flatbreads or pitta
breads into bite-sized pieces. Lay in a single layer
on a baking sheet, drizzle with oil, and grill for
2–3 minutes, shaking the tray halfway through
until crisp and golden. Keep your eye on the bread
so that it doesn't burn. Remove and allow to cool
to room temperature.

In a large serving bowl, combine the parsley,
tomatoes, and pomegranate seeds. Add the
crunchy bread, pile the charred onions on top with
their juices, and crumble over the feta.

# LIME, CHILLI & CHEESE
★
# CORN SKEWERS

Corn served like this is ever popular in Mexico and India.
It's the kind of street food you eat on holiday and vow
to recreate at home – and now you know just how. Serve
with plenty of napkins!

 SERVES 4

 TAKES 20 minutes

4 corn on the cob, husks removed
2 tbsp butter, softened
1 lime, zested
1 tsp chilli flakes
handful coriander (cilantro), finely
    chopped
50g/1¾oz feta, crumbled

Heat a barbeque or griddle pan to high. Carefully push a skewer into each corn cob. Cook the corn for 10–15 minutes, using the skewer as a handle to regularly turn the cobs.

Meanwhile, in a bowl, mix the butter and lime zest with the chilli flakes and coriander. Cut the lime into wedges and set aside.

Once the corn is charred in places and tender, remove the cobs from the heat. Spread the butter over each one, sprinkle with the feta, and squeeze over the lime juice before eating.

TOUM & HERB

★

# HALLOUMI & PINK PICKLES

Toum is a deliciously creamy garlic sauce that partners
perfectly with salty halloumi, fresh herbs, and pretty pink
pickled turnips. This kebab looks as good as it tastes.

SERVES 2

TAKES 20 minutes

2 pickled pink turnips, cut
    into wedges
½ red onion, thinly sliced
250g/9oz halloumi
1 large, thick flatbread or
    2 thin flatbreads
handful flat-leaf parsley,
    roughly chopped
handful cherry tomatoes,
    roughly chopped
1 Lebanese cucumber, cut
    into batons
salt and freshly ground
    black pepper
**For the toum**
2 garlic cloves, crushed
juice and zest ½ lemon
1 egg white
200ml/7fl oz/generous ¾ cup
    olive oil
**To serve**
2 large pickled chillies
½ lemon, cut into wedges

Start by making the toum. Place the garlic, lemon
juice and zest, egg white, and oil into a high-sided
jar or container. Use a stick blender to combine
the ingredients, moving the blender up and down
until the ingredients have emulsified – it will
take a matter of seconds. Season and add about
2 tablespoons warm water if the toum looks
very thick; it should be the consistency of loose
mayonnaise. Set aside.

Put the turnips into a bowl with the onion and
pour over a little of the pickling juice, toss to coat,
and leave to stand.

Meanwhile, heat a griddle pan to high. Cut the
halloumi into 8 slices and cook for 1–2 minutes on
each side, or until softened and golden brown.

Spread the flatbread(s) with 1–2 tablespoons of the
toum, followed by the parsley, halloumi, cherry
tomatoes, cucumber, and finally the pickled turnips
and onion. Serve with a pickled chilli and lemon
wedge for squeezing.

Any leftover toum can be stored in an airtight
container in the fridge for up to 2 days.

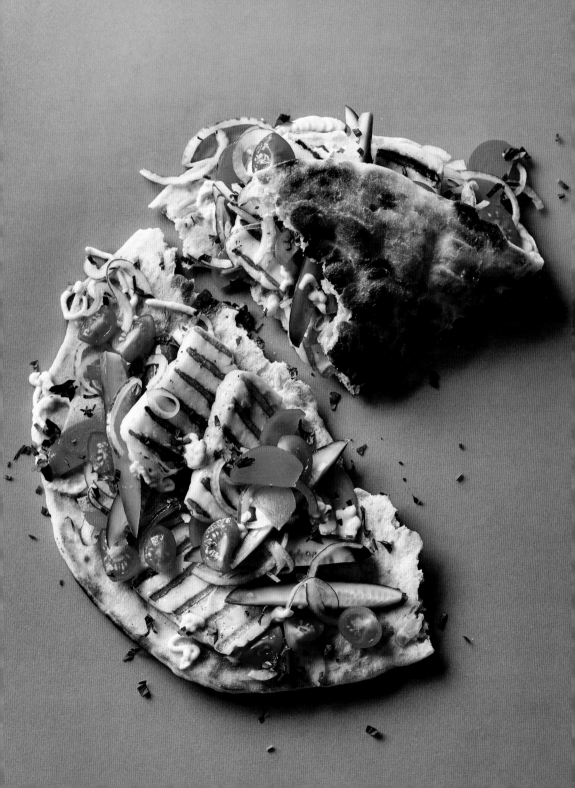

PORCINI-SAUCED

★

# WILD MUSHROOM KEBABS

Wild mushrooms are a seasonal treat. If you can't get your hands on wild ones, use chestnut mushrooms; the porcini sauce will elevate even the most mundane variety.

SERVES 4

TAKES 20 minutes, plus standing time

650g/1lb 7oz mixed wild mushrooms
75g/2½oz butter, melted
freshly ground black pepper
**For the porcini sauce**
25g/scant 1oz dried porcini
2 shallots, finely chopped
2 tbsp thyme leaves
2 garlic cloves, crushed
50ml/2fl oz/scant ¼ cup Marsala
50ml/2fl oz/scant ¼ cup double (heavy) cream
mashed potato, to serve

First get the sauce started. Soak the porcini in 500ml/17½fl oz/2 cups hot water. Cover and leave to stand for 20 minutes.

Preheat the grill to high. Remove any dirt and grit from the wild mushrooms using a damp cloth or pastry brush. Halve any large mushrooms, then thread them onto 8 small skewers. Lay in a single layer on a baking sheet, brush generously with half the melted butter, and season with black pepper. Cook for 8 minutes, turning every minute or so, until the mushrooms are golden. Turn off the grill but leave the mushrooms under it to keep warm.

To make the sauce, tip the remaining butter into a frying pan, add the shallots and thyme, and cook on a medium heat for 5 minutes until really soft and beginning to take on a little colour. Add the garlic and cook for a further minute. Drain the porcini, reserving the soaking liquor. Roughly chop the porcini, then add them to the pan with 200ml/7fl oz/generous ¾ cup of the liquor. Increase the heat, pour in the Marsala, and bubble for 5 minutes until slightly reduced. Swirl in the cream and plenty of seasoning. Remove from the heat.

Spoon the sauce over the mushroom kebabs and serve with creamy mashed potato.

## CRISPY FRIED EGG &

★

# AVOCADO BREAKFAST KEBABS

---

Kebab for breakfast often means an early-morning stumble into the arms of a takeaway, a little the worse for wear. But not any more! This breakfast naan is packed with healthy, tasty ingredients with zero guilt attached.

 SERVES 2

 TAKES 10 minutes

2 naan breads
2 tbsp olive oil
1 large avocado, halved, stoned
   and thickly sliced
100g/3½oz cherry vine tomatoes
2 eggs
2 tbsp chilli jam
handful coriander (cilantro),
   roughly chopped

Heat the naan breads according to packet instructions until hot and fluffy.

Meanwhile, heat a griddle pan to high. Drizzle about 1 teaspoon of the oil over the avocado slices and tomatoes, then cook for 3–5 minutes, flipping the avocado halfway through cooking to char both sides and give the tomatoes a shake – you want them to soften but still hold their shape.

Heat the remaining oil in a frying pan. Crack the eggs into the hot oil and cook to your liking.

Spread the hot naan breads with the chilli jam, slide a fried egg onto each, followed by the griddled avocado slices and tomatoes. Finish with the coriander, roll up, and eat.

# KALE CRISPS & COURGETTES

You can make all the components of this wonderful kebab in advance and unveil at the table for maximum impact. It's a combination of fabulous flavours but also textures that will have your veggie friends begging for the recipe.

 SERVES 4

 TAKES 20 minutes

400g/14oz can cannellini beans, drained and rinsed

3 medium cooked beetroots, drained and roughly chopped

3 tbsp Greek yogurt

1 garlic clove, roughly chopped

2 large courgettes (zucchini), cut into 1cm/¾in slices

2 tbsp olive oil

100g/3½oz kale, tough stalks removed

1 tsp paprika

½ tsp cumin seeds

25g/scant 1oz roasted hazelnuts, roughly chopped

2 tbsp white wine vinegar

1 tsp caster (superfine) sugar

2 banana shallots, very thinly sliced

salt and freshly ground black pepper

4–8 flatbreads, to serve

Tip the cannellini beans into the bowl of a food processor with the beetroots, yogurt, and garlic. Whizz until smooth. Season, then scrape out into a bowl, cover, and set aside.

Heat a griddle pan to high. Brush the courgettes with a little olive oil, then cook for 5 minutes, turning halfway through, or until charred and starting to soften slightly. Remove and set aside.

Preheat the grill to high. In a large bowl, toss the kale with the remaining olive oil, the paprika, and cumin seeds. Season, then lay in a single layer on a baking sheet. Grill for 3–4 minutes, or until the kale is starting to char at the edges. Turn and char the other side for 1 minute, scatter over the hazelnuts, and toast for a few seconds until fragrant. Set aside.

In a small bowl, mix the vinegar and sugar to dissolve the granules, tip in the shallots, and stir to coat. Leave to stand for a few minutes.

To serve, heat the flatbreads, spread with the beany beetroot dip, top with slices of griddled courgette, crisp kale and hazelnuts, and pickled shallots.

132

Vegetarian Kebabs

## CHOPPED RADISH SALAD

★

# FALAFEL & SPICED YOGURT

Good-quality ready-made falafel make for such a quick
and easy kebab, perfect for a filling lunch or tasty dinner.
Once you're in on the secret, you will never revert
to your local takeaway.

 SERVES 4

 TAKES 15 minutes

2 x 200g/7oz packets ready-made
  falafel
200g/7oz radishes, finely sliced
2 Lebanese cucumbers, finely
  chopped
2 large tomatoes, deseeded and
  finely chopped
1 baby gem lettuce, shredded
**For the spiced yogurt**
½ tsp cumin seeds
½ tsp coriander seeds
200g/7oz natural yogurt
1 garlic clove, crushed
handful mint, finely chopped
1 tsp white wine vinegar
pinch salt
**To serve**
4 white pitta breads
chilli sauce
natural yogurt

Start by making the spiced yogurt. Heat a frying
pan, then add the cumin and coriander seeds.
When the seeds start to pop and become fragrant,
remove them from the heat and tip into a bowl.
Crush in a pestle and mortar if you have one. Add
the yogurt, garlic, mint, vinegar, and salt. Stir to
combine, then set aside.

Heat the falafel according to packet instructions.
Three minutes before the end of cooking, put the
pitta breads in the oven to heat through.

Combine the radishes, cucumbers, and tomatoes
together in a bowl. Split the pittas along the top
edge to form a large pocket, spread with the spiced
yogurt, add 3–4 falafels per pitta, stuff in some
lettuce, and top with the mixed salad. Serve with
chilli sauce and extra yogurt.

# CHARRED

★

# BABY AUBERGINES

Thread the baby aubergines onto skewers so they won't roll through the gaps of the barbeque. Perfect summer food, cook over a flame to give a wonderful smoky flavour. If it's not barbeque weather, a griddle pan will suffice.

 SERVES 4

 TAKES 20 minutes

16 baby aubergines (eggplants), halved lengthways
1 tbsp olive oil
50g/1¾oz butter
3 tbsp tomato purée
2 tsp smoked paprika
1 tsp Turkish pepper flakes
200g/7oz Greek yogurt
1 garlic clove, crushed
8 flatbreads
100g/3½oz rocket

Heat a griddle pan or barbeque to high. Thread the aubergines onto 4 large skewers, brush with the oil, and cook for 3–5 minutes on each side, or until charred and softened.

Meanwhile, melt the butter in a small pan, then add the tomato purée, smoked paprika, and Turkish pepper flakes. Remove from the heat after about 2 minutes.

In a bowl, mix the yogurt and garlic. Heat the flatbreads in a warm oven or on the barbeque for a few seconds. Spread the flatbreads with the garlic yogurt, lay over the charred aubergines, add a handful of rocket leaves, drizzle with the tomato butter sauce, and serve.

# CHARGRILLED
★
# MUSHROOMS & MANGO SALSA

---

Portobellos' size and natural meatiness mean they can
stand the high heat of a barbeque and beautifully take
on all the smoky flavours. These mushrooms are great
wrapped in a flatbread with salsa or in a burger bun.

 SERVES 2

 TAKES 15 minutes,
plus marinating

8 portobello mushrooms
75g/2½oz mature Cheddar, grated
3 spring onions (scallions), finely
chopped
1 red chilli, deseeded and finely
chopped
freshly ground black pepper
**For the salsa**
1 ripe mango, peeled and diced
1 spring onion (scallion), finely
chopped
2 medium tomatoes, deseeded and
finely chopped
2 tbsp jalapeño chillies from a jar,
finely chopped
juice 1 lime
handful coriander (cilantro), finely
chopped
4 flour tortillas, to serve

Clean off any dirt from the mushrooms using a
pastry brush. Remove the stalks of the mushrooms
and discard.

Heat a griddle pan or barbeque to high. Place the
mushrooms cup-side down and cook for 2 minutes.
Mix the cheese, spring onions, and chilli with some
black pepper. Flip the mushrooms over in the
pan, then fill the cup of each mushroom with the
cheese filling. Cook for a further 3 minutes until the
mushrooms are soft and the cheese is molten.

Meanwhile, make the salsa. In a bowl, combine
the mango, spring onion, tomatoes, jalapeños,
1 teaspoon of the pickling water, the lime juice,
and coriander.

Heat the tortillas on the griddle pan, then pile a
filled mushroom and salsa on top, roll up, and eat.

# ASPARAGUS, ROMESCO &
★
# GRIDDLED SPRING ONIONS

This recipe was inspired by calçots – a type of spring onion resembling a leek – that are barbequed and dunked into a smoky, pepper-and-nut sauce during competitive eating contests throughout Catalonia.

 SERVES 4

 TAKES 30 minutes

3 bunches (about 12 onions) large
  spring onions (scallions)
12 asparagus spears
olive oil, for brushing
**For the romesco sauce**
90ml/3fl oz/scant ½ cup olive oil
50g/1¾oz roasted hazelnuts
3 roasted red (bell) peppers from
  a jar, drained and roughly
  chopped
1 tbsp red wine vinegar
1 tbsp sweet smoked paprika
½ garlic clove, crushed
**To serve**
4 flatbreads
75g/2½oz Manchego

Heat a barbeque or griddle pan to high. Cut off any straggly green ends and the roots of the spring onions, then halve them lengthways. Trim the tough ends of the asparagus. Lay the spring onions and asparagus in a straight line on the barbeque or griddle pan, and brush with a little oil. Cook for 4–5 minutes, turning halfway through, until charred and tender.

To make the romesco sauce, tip the oil, hazelnuts, red peppers, vinegar, paprika, and garlic into the bowl of a food processor and pulse until smooth. Transfer to a bowl.

Warm the flatbreads on the barbeque or griddle, spoon over a generous dollop of romesco sauce, pile on the spring onions and asparagus, and shave over the Manchego. Serve immediately.

★

# CARROT HUMMUS & PISTOU

Buy a lovely bunch of leafy carrots for this recipe. Here, the tops are made into a bright green pistou and the roots roasted to bring out all of their amazing sweetness. Hummus addicts will be hooked on this carrot variation.

 SERVES 4

 TAKES 1 hour

400g/14oz bunch carrots with tops
5–6 tbsp olive oil
2 tsp cumin seeds
1 tbsp za'atar
handful flat-leaf parsley
2 garlic cloves, bashed
juice and zest 1 lemon
400g/14oz can chickpeas
   (garbanzo beans), drained
   and rinsed
2 tbsp tahini
4 large fluffy flatbreads
100g/3½oz feta
salt and freshly ground black
   pepper

Preheat the oven to 190°C/170°C fan/gas 5. Cut the leafy green tops from the carrots and reserve. Halve any fat carrots lengthways, then tip into a roasting tin and toss with 1 tablespoon of the oil, the cumin seeds, and 1 teaspoon of the za'atar. Season, then roast for 45 minutes, stirring halfway through until golden and tender.

Meanwhile, make the pistou. Wash the carrot tops really well to remove any grit, pat dry, then roughly chop on a chopping board. Add the parsley, 1 garlic clove, and the lemon zest. Run the knife over the ingredients until really finely chopped. Scrape into a bowl and add 2–3 tablespoons of the oil and a splash of lemon juice to make a spoonable sauce.

Tip the chickpeas into a food processor with the remaining garlic clove, 2 tablespoons of the oil, the remaining lemon juice, and the tahini. Roughly chop one-third of the roasted carrots and add into the processor with 50ml/1¾fl oz/scant ¼ cup cold water, and pulse until smooth. Season to taste.

Heat the flatbreads in a warm oven, spread with the carrot hummus, lay some roasted carrots on top, and spoon over the pistou. Scatter with the feta and remaining za'atar.

# TANDOORI

★

# PANEER & MIXED PEPPERS

---

These kebabs are especially good if you cook them over the
barbeque. Charring the peppers makes them so sweet,
and they work perfectly with the salty, spiced paneer. Use
a variety of peppers for the most vibrant colour.

 SERVES 4

TAKES 15 minutes,
plus marinating

4 garlic cloves, crushed
5cm/2in piece ginger, peeled and
  finely grated
juice ½ lemon
300g/10oz natural yogurt
2 tbsp sunflower oil
1 tbsp paprika
1 tbsp ground cumin
1 tbsp garam masala
1 tbsp ground turmeric
1 tsp hot chilli powder
2 x 225g/8oz packets paneer, cut
  into 2.5cm/1in cubes
2 red onions
2 red (bell) peppers
2 green (bell) peppers
salt and freshly ground black
  pepper

In a medium bowl, mix the garlic, ginger, lemon
juice, yogurt, oil, and spices together. Season, then
add the paneer and toss to coat. Cover and set
aside to marinate for 30 minutes.

Meanwhile, cut the onions into eighths. Cut the
peppers into 2.5cm/1in cubes. Set aside.

To make the raita (ingredients overleaf), halve the
cucumber lengthways, then scrape out and discard
the seeds using a teaspoon, and cut the flesh into
small dice. Tip the yogurt into a bowl, and add the
cucumber, mint, and chilli. Cover and chill
until required.

Lift the paneer out of the marinade. Thread onto 4
long skewers with the onions and mixed peppers,
brushing over any excess marinade. Preheat the
grill, barbeque, or griddle pan to high. Once
hot, cook the skewers for 8–10 minutes, turning

ingredients and method continue overleaf...

★ ★ ★ ★ ★ ★ ★ ★ ★ ★ ★ ★ ★ ★ ★ ★ ★ ★ ★ ★ ★ ★ ★ ★ ★ ★ ★ ★ ★ ★ ★ ★ ★ ★ ★ ★

# TANDOORI PANEER

continued...

**For the raita**

½ cucumber

300g/10oz natural yogurt

large handful mint leaves, finely
     chopped

1 green finger chilli, deseeded and
     finely chopped

**To serve**

4 chapattis

½ lemon, cut into wedges

frequently until the peppers and onions are charred in places and the paneer is soft and golden.

Warm the chapattis in a hot oven for a few minutes, then slide the paneer and veggies off their skewers with a fork and dollop on the raita. Serve with lemon wedges for squeezing.

# WHIPPED FETA WITH
★
# SQUASH PATTIES

Whipping feta elevates this humble, salty cheese to more than just something you sprinkle on salads at the last minute. Whipped, it is reinvented into a luxuriously smooth spread. Keep some in the fridge for all your kebab-eating escapades. It goes particularly well with these sweet and spicy squash patties.

 SERVES 4

 TAKES 55 minutes, plus chilling

### For the squash patties
600g/1lb 5oz butternut squash, seeds removed and cut into 2.5cm/1in cubes
3 tbsp olive oil
2 tsp cumin seeds
3 garlic cloves, roughly chopped
1 tsp ground coriander
400g/14oz can chickpeas, drained and rinsed
1 red chilli, deseeded and finely chopped
large handful coriander (cilantro), leaves and stems separated
50g/1¾oz fresh breadcrumbs
salt and freshly ground black pepper

Start by making the squash patties. Preheat the oven to 200°C/180°C fan/gas 6. Put the squash on a baking tray – leave the skin on because it adds a nice texture. Drizzle over 1 tablespoon of the olive oil and scatter with the cumin seeds, then toss to coat. Roast for 40 minutes, stirring halfway through, until the squash is tender and caramelized in places.

Scrape the squash into the bowl of a food processor. Add the garlic along with the ground coriander, chickpeas, chilli, and plenty of seasoning. Roughly chop the coriander stalks and add them to the food processor with the breadcrumbs and plenty of salt and black pepper. Pulse until combined but not smooth – you want to keep some texture.

Divide the mixture into 12 equal portions, then using damp hands, shape the mixture into little patties. Then place them on a baking tray, and chill for 30 minutes.

ingredients and method continue overleaf...

★ ★ ★ ★ ★ ★ ★ ★ ★ ★ ★ ★ ★ ★ ★ ★ ★ ★ ★ ★ ★ ★ ★ ★ ★ ★ ★ ★ ★ ★ ★ ★ ★ ★ ★ ★ ★

# SQUASH PATTIES

continued...

For the whipped feta
200g/7oz feta, crumbled
2 tbsp olive oil
½ garlic clove, crushed
50g/1¾oz Greek yogurt

To serve
4 flatbreads
1 small red onion, thinly sliced

Meanwhile, make the whipped feta. Put the cheese, oil, garlic, and yogurt into a food processor and whizz until smooth. Scrape out and chill until needed.

Heat the remaining oil in a large frying pan over a medium heat. Once hot, add the patties and cook for about 5 minutes, gently turning halfway through, and cook until golden and piping hot.

Warm the flatbreads, spoon the whipped feta over the surface, top with the patties, red onion, and chopped coriander leaves.

TAHINI-DRESSED

★

# BLACKENED CAULIFLOWER

Gone are the days of soggy, grey cauliflower. This kebab is all about the blackened florets, wonderfully crisp at the edges and velvety soft in the middle.

 SERVES 2

 TAKES 50 minutes

1 large cauliflower, broken into
   florets, small leaves reserved
4 tbsp olive oil
4 garlic cloves, unpeeled
2 red onions, cut into wedges
   through the root
handful golden raisins
handful pitted green olives,
   roughly chopped
2 tbsp tahini
juice ½ lemon
salt
2–4 wholemeal pitta breads
75g/2½oz Greek yogurt

Preheat the oven to 220°C/200°C fan/gas 7. Toss the cauliflower florets with 3 tablespoons of the oil on a large baking tray and roast for 20 minutes. After this time, add the garlic, onions, and cauliflower leaves and stir to combine. Roast for a further 20–25 minutes until the cauliflower is charred at the edges and tender, and the garlic and onions are softened. Remove from the oven, pick out the garlic cloves, and set aside. Add the raisins and olives to the cauliflower.

Squeeze out the flesh from the roasted garlic using the back of a knife and tip into a small bowl. Add the tahini, lemon juice, remaining oil, a little salt, and 2–3 tablespoons cold water to make a fluid but not too runny dressing.

Toast the pitta breads, then split them in half. Spread with the yogurt, pile with the blackened cauliflower mixture, and spoon over the tahini dressing.

# CORIANDER & PUMPKIN SEED
★
# SWEET POTATO

Here, the sweet, soft potato flesh, with its crispy charred exterior, is perfect with the smooth, spicy pumpkin seed salsa – you have to try it to believe it. Everyone who has eaten this loved the combination of flavours and textures.

 SERVES 2

 TAKES 1 hour

3 medium sweet potatoes
50g/1¾oz pumpkin seeds
juice 2 limes
2 tbsp olive oil
2 jalepeño peppers, deseeded and finely chopped
1 large avocado
½ garlic clove, crushed
large handful coriander (cilantro)
salt and freshly ground black pepper
**To serve**
4 corn tortillas
soured cream

Preheat the oven to 220°C/200°C fan/gas 7. Put the sweet potatoes on a baking sheet and bake for 45–50 minutes until tender.

Meanwhile, make the pumpkin seed salsa. Put the pumpkin seeds on a baking tray and cook in the oven for 6 minutes, stirring halfway through, then remove from the oven and allow to cool. Put three-quarters of the seeds into the bowl of a food processor with the lime juice, oil, and jalepeño peppers. Add the avocado, garlic, and most of the coriander, reserving a few leaves for garnish. Add a splash of cold water – enough to loosen the mixture into a smooth, spoonable sauce – you don't want it too runny, then whizz to combine. Season and set aside.

Preheat the grill to high. When the sweet potatoes are tender, flash them under the grill until the skin is charred and crisp.

Warm the tortillas. Thickly slice the potatoes in their skins and serve in a tortilla with the salsa and some soured cream. Scatter over the reserved crunchy pumpkin seeds and garnish with chopped coriander leaves.

# FIG & HALLOUMI
★
# SKEWERS

These skewers can go either way: sweet enough to serve as
a dessert or savoury enough to serve with piles of garlicky
herb labneh (see page 67) and flatbreads for a light lunch.
However you serve these skewers, make sure the halloumi
is still hot and soft and the figs juicy.

 SERVES 4

TAKES 10 minutes

8 small, firm, ripe figs
250g/9oz halloumi, cut into
   2.5cm/1in cubes
1 tbsp clear honey
1 tbsp finely chopped mint

Cut a small cross through each of the figs, making
sure you do not cut all the way through to the
base. Thread onto 4 small skewers, alternating with
halloumi cubes. Transfer to a baking tray.

Preheat the grill to high. Grill the skewers for 3
minutes until the figs are soft and juicy and the
halloumi golden in places and hot.

Use a spatula to transfer to serving plates. Drizzle
with the honey and sprinkle with the mint.

# PICKLED CARROTS &
★
# MISO AUBERGINE

Miso is the ultimate umami food and makes everything taste great. It's worth keeping a jar in the fridge at all times as it can be brushed over most things to transform them into a tasty treat.

 SERVES 2

 TAKES 25 minutes

2 tbsp miso
1 tbsp sesame oil, plus a drizzle
1 tbsp clear honey
1 large aubergine (eggplant), cut into 3cm/1in dice

**For the pickled carrots**
2 tbsp rice wine vinegar
1 tbsp caster sugar
1 large carrot, sliced with a julienne peeler or potato peeler
1 tbsp toasted sesame seeds
2 spring onions (scallions), shredded
boiled rice, to serve

Start by making the pickled carrots. In a bowl, mix the vinegar with the sugar and 1 tablespoon warm water, and stir to dissolve the sugar. Add the carrot, then set aside.

Preheat the grill to high. In a bowl, mix the miso, sesame oil, honey, and 1 tablespoon cold water. Add the aubergine and toss to coat. Thread the aubergine cubes onto 4 small skewers, reserving the marinade. Lightly grease a baking tray with a drizzle of oil, lay the skewers in a single layer, and grill for 20 minutes until soft, sticky, and dark, turning halfway through and brushing with the reserved marinade.

Scatter the skewers with the sesame seeds, and serve with the pickled carrots and spring onions over a bowl of boiled rice.

# SWEET

★

# KEBABS

# MARSHMALLOW
★
# S'MORES WITH CHOCOLATE

Gooey blistered marshmallow sandwiched between crunchy biscuit. Don't be tempted to thread too many marshmallows onto each skewer – you want them all to be hot, soft, and sticky so they melt into the chocolate biscuit. Be prepared to get very messy with these skewers.

  SERVES 4

TAKES 5 minutes

8 marshmallows
8 dark chocolate biscuits (I used Bahlsen Choco Leibniz Dark Chocolate biscuits)
**For the hot chocolate**
600ml/1 pint/2½ cups whole milk
pinch salt
100g/3½oz dark chocolate, roughly chopped

Start by making the hot chocolate. Put the milk into a small pan and heat gently. Once boiling, remove from the heat and add the salt. Divide the chocolate between 4 mugs, top with the hot milk, and stir to melt the chocolate.

Take 4 small skewers and thread 2 marshmallows onto each. Toast the marshmallows over an open flame or under a hot grill until charred and sticky – be careful not to touch the marshmallows as they will be very hot. Remove from the heat. Take two biscuits and sandwich one marshmallow skewer in between, pull the skewer out, and repeat with the remaining skewers and biscuits. Eat your s'mores with a mug of hot chocolate for an indulgent treat.

LIME & CHILLI

★

# GRIDDLED PINEAPPLE

Sweet, ripe pineapple goes perfectly with zingy lime and spicy chilli. This hot, juicy kebab is delicious served with a scoop of vanilla ice cream. And if you like it boozy, add a slug of dark rum to the syrup.

 SERVES 4

 TAKES 15 minutes

1 large ripe pineapple, unpeeled
**For the lime and chilli drizzle**
100g/3½oz soft brown sugar
juice and zest 2 limes
1 red chilli, deseeded and finely
   chopped
vanilla ice cream, to serve

Start by making the drizzle. Put the sugar into a small pan with 75ml/2½fl oz/⅓ cup cold water and the lime juice. Heat gently until the sugar has dissolved, then increase the heat and bubble for 6–8 minutes until the liquid is slightly reduced and syrupy. Remove from the heat and allow to cool.

Cut the pineapple into quarters lengthways, then cut each quarter into 1.5cm/¾in slices widthways. Heat a griddle pan or barbeque to high and dry the surface of the pineapple with kitchen paper – this will prevent it from sticking to the grill. Push the pineapple wedges onto 4 skewers, transfer to the griddle, and cook for 2–3 minutes on each side, or until charred and hot.

Remove from the heat and pour the drizzle over the pineapple skewers. Scatter with the lime zest and chilli, and serve with a scoop of vanilla ice cream.

# CINNAMON

# STICKY APPLES

The ultimate sweet kebab, the sweet, spiced bread is perfect
to mop up the sticky apple juices. All the flavours of apple
pie in kebab form.

 SERVES 4

 TAKES 20 minutes

25g/scant 1oz unsalted butter,
   softened
2 dessert apples, cored and cut
   into 8 wedges each
5 tbsp soft brown sugar
50ml/1¾fl oz/scant ¼ cup
   double (heavy) cream
1 plain naan bread or other
   thick flatbread
1 tsp ground cinnamon
½ tsp mixed spice
vanilla ice cream, to serve

Heat half the butter in a large non-stick frying
pan over a medium heat. Once bubbling, throw in
the apple wedges and cook for 5 minutes, turning
frequently, until they start to take on some colour.
Add 4 tablespoons of the sugar to the frying
pan, increase the heat to high, shake the pan to
dissolve the sugar, pour in the cream, and bubble
for 2 minutes, continuing to gently shake the pan
until the sauce is thick and the apples are tender.
Remove from the heat.

Preheat the grill to high. Sprinkle a few drops of
water over the surface of the naan bread, grill for
1 minute, then flip over and grill for a further
minute. Spread one side of the bread with the
remaining butter. Mix the remaining tablespoon of
sugar with the spices, then sprinkle over the bread.
Return to the grill for 2 minutes, or until the sugar
starts to crystallize. Remove from the heat, place
the naan bread onto a board and pour over the
sticky apple wedges. Cut into pieces and serve with
a scoop of good vanilla ice cream.

# GRIDDLED BANANAS
★
# WITH SOFT-SERVE

You will love this super-simple ice cream so much. It has to be the quickest, easiest dessert ever – and it's perfect for using up those brown bananas that languish at the bottom of the fruit bowl. Barbequing bananas makes them intensely sweet and gooey.

 SERVES 4

 TAKES 15 minutes, plus freezing

8 small ripe bananas
3 tbsp tahini
2 tbsp maple syrup, plus extra
   to serve
pinch salt
1 tbsp toasted sesame seeds,
   to serve

Peel and slice 4 of the bananas into 0.5cm/¼in pieces. Lay them in a single layer on a baking sheet and freeze for 2 hours, or until the banana slices are frozen solid. Remove from the freezer, tip into the bowl of a food processor, and add the tahini, maple syrup, and salt. Whizz until all the ingredients are combined and the mixture looks thick and creamy. Scrape into a freezer-proof container and place in the freezer until ready to use. Remove from the freezer 10 minutes before you want to scoop.

Heat a barbeque or griddle pan to high and cook the remaining bananas in their skins, turning a couple of times until the skins are blackened all over – it should take about 10 minutes.

To serve, peel back the skins and serve with a scoop of banana ice cream, and sprinkle with the toasted sesame seeds and extra maple syrup, if liked.

CHOCOLATEY

★

# BERRY SKEWERS

Quick and easy fruit kebabs are such a crowd pleaser. Use any fruit you have to hand on these skewers – grapes, mango, and pineapple all work really well. Go as mad as you like with the sprinkles too, or keep it simple with just some good-quality chocolate.

 SERVES 4

TAKES 15 minutes

16 strawberries, hulled
16 raspberries
16 blackberries
50g/1¾oz white chocolate, roughly chopped
50g/1¾oz dark chocolate, roughly chopped
25g/scant 1oz roasted hazelnuts, finely chopped (optional)

Line a baking sheet with baking paper. Thread the berries onto 8 small skewers, being careful not to squash the softer fruit. Lay the skewers onto the prepared baking sheet and transfer to the fridge to chill.

Meanwhile, put the white and dark chocolates into two separate heatproof bowls. Melt the chocolate in 20-second bursts in the microwave, or set the bowls, one at a time, over a pan of barely simmering water (taking care that the base of the bowl does not touch the water), stirring until melted. Remove from the heat and allow to cool for a few moments.

Remove the berry skewers from the fridge, drizzle the skewers with the white and dark chocolates, and scatter with the nuts. The chocolate should set quickly as the fruit is cold. Serve immediately, or return to the fridge and chill until ready to serve.

# HONEY, PISTACHIO & ORANGE
## ★
# GRILLED PEACHES

Peaches are so deliciously sweet and juicy when cooked this way; their juices mingle with the honey and orange perfectly. This makes a rather stylish dessert in minutes.

 SERVES 4

TAKES 10 minutes

2 large ripe, firm peaches, stoned and quartered
2 tbsp clear honey
zest 1 orange and flesh chopped
200g/7oz Greek yogurt
25g/scant 1oz roasted pistachios, finely chopped

Heat a griddle pan to high, then place the peach quarters, cut-side down, and cook for 2 minutes. Gently flip and cook the remaining cut half for 2 minutes. Remove the peaches from the heat, transfer to a plate, drizzle with the honey, and sprinkle over the orange zest and chopped flesh.

Divide the yogurt between 4 bowls, spoon over the peaches, orange pieces, and any juices, and scatter with the pistachios.

# INDEX

yogurt 135
chorizo sausages
   Garlic & lemon squid with chorizo 110
   Piquillo pepper & chorizo skewers 54
Chutney, Onion 38
Cinnamon sticky apples 164
cod
   Garlic & lemon cod & peach skewers 94
Coriander & pumpkin seed sweet potato 152
corn on the cob
   Lime, chilli & cheese corn skewers 125
Couscous 16
Crispy fried egg & avocado breakfast
   kebabs 130
cucumbers
   Cucumber noodles 71
   Ezme salad 30
   Kachumba salad 24
   Raita 109, 145, 146

# D

duck
   Duck satay skewers 74
   Sticky Chinese five spice duck 71

# E

eggs
   Crispy fried egg & avocado breakfast
     kebabs 130
   Ezme salad 30

# F

falafel
   Chopped radish salad, falafel & spiced
     yogurt 135
Fennel & chilli chicken & orange salad 86
feta cheese
   Griddled red onion wedges 122
   Lime, chilli & cheese corn skewers 125
   Whipped feta with squash patties 147–9
Fig & halloumi skewers 155
fish dishes
   Anchovy & tomato paprika
     flatbreads 98
   Avocado and sea bass ceviche 106
   Harissa sardines 97
   Lemon monkfish skewers 117
     Smoked trout with dill pickles 113

Sumac & lemon mackerel 105
Tandoori salmon 109
Thyme, garlic & lemon cod & peach
   skewers 94
Tuna with wasabi mayo 92
Yuzu, soy & honey salmon skewers 102
fruit
   Chocolatey berry skewers 168
   Cinnamon sticky apples 164
   Couscous 16
   Fennel & chilli chicken & orange salad 86
   Griddled bananas with soft serve 167
   Honey, pistachio & orange grilled
     peaches 170
   Lime & chilli griddled pineapple 162
   Mango salsa 139
   Sweet sticky lamb sosatie 51
   Thyme, garlic & lemon cod & peach
     skewers 94

# G

Garlic & lemon cod & peach skewers 94
Garlic & lemon squid with chorizo 110
Garlic yogurt 136
goat
   Rice & beans curried goat 17–19

# H

halloumi
   Fig & halloumi skewers 155
   Toum & herb halloumi & pink pickles 126
haricot beans
   Smoky baked beans 46
Harissa sardines 97
Herby chicken wings 85
Honey, pistachio & orange grilled peaches 170

# I

ice cream
   Griddled bananas with soft serve 167
Iskender kebabs, Lamb 48

# J

Jerk pork & apple slaw 26

# K

Kachumba salad 24

# ACKNOWLEDGEMENTS

This book is everything I love, it is a riot of colour and pattern, fun and filled with fuss-free, super-tasty, great-looking food.

Sarah Lavelle and the Quadrille team, it's like you knew I'd love working on this book before I did. Thank you so much for asking me to be a part of the *Posh* series.

Faith, Alexander and Gemma, it looks good enough to eat. Thank you all for creating such a visual treat.

Jess Dennison thank you so much for your thorough testing, eating and feedback.

Leigh Clark, you're ace. And Curt, you make life taste better!

3 1333 04599 3977